How to improve your
CROCHET
TECHNIQUES

CAVENDISH HOUSE

Here at last is a clear but comprehensive guide in colour to the traditional popular craft of crochet. With a simple hook and a ball of yarn you can create beautiful stitches which can be used in thousands of ways for the family and home. If you're a beginner you'll find all the basic steps you need to start, and if you are an experienced crochet worker there are over a hundred stitches and techniques which you will be able to use, including Irish crochet; Tunisian crochet; chevrons; Aran: patterns, stripes and checks; surface crochet; blocks; borders and edgings, and much, much more. In addition there are two beginners' garments — a useful 'his and hers' cardigan and an attractive patchwork slip-on, plus five simple accessories for you to make.

Contents

Editor: Nicky Hayden
Crochet editor: Pam Dawson
Crochet consultant: Jean Litchfield
Art Editor: Caroline Austin
Cover photograph: Alan Duns
Photography: Alan Duns; Bruce Scott
pp. 5-9, 12, 23, 29; Peter Watkins p. 12
(bottom)
Victoria and Albert Museum/John
Freeman Ltd p.3.
Illustrations: Barbara Firth

Accessories
Page 64: Buckle from a selection at
the John Lewis Partnership, London

Published by Marshall Cavendish Books Limited
58 Old Compton Street
London W1V 5PA

First printing 1975 (softback)
Second printing 1983 (hardback)

Printed by L.E.G.O., Vicenza, Italy

ISBN 0 86307 062 0

Crochet know-how

Crochet is a rewarding and practical craft, both simple and quick to work once the basic steps have been mastered. Just as with knitting, however, there is a correct way to produce the best results and tricks-of-the-trade to give a professional finish.

If you are interested in learning how to crochet or would like to add to your knowledge about some of the more unusual crochet techniques, the following pages will prove invaluable. The beginner will find that she can soon master the basic steps which are set out clearly and simply and produce her first garment—the crochet cardigan has been designed specifically with the beginner in mind.

The more experienced crochet worker will find many ways to improve her skills and dozens of beautiful stitches, which she may be tempted to adapt to her own designs.

The tools required
A rigid metal centimetre/inch rule
Scissors
Blunt-ended sewing needles
Rustless steel pins
Polythene bag in which to keep work clean
Iron and ironing pad or blanket
Cotton cloths suitable for use when pressing

Know your hooks
Crochet hooks are now available in metric sizes and since the hook does not hold any stitches but merely the working loop, they are all produced to the same, easily manageable length. The larger the metric number, the larger the size of the hook.

Tunisian crochet hooks are also available in metric sizes but because the working method for Tunisian crochet requires a number of stitches to be held on the hook, they are produced in varying lengths to accommodate the correct number of stitches required. Again, the larger the metric number the larger the hook.

ISR hooks	old Wool sizes	ISR hooks	old Cotton sizes
7.00	2	2.00	$1\frac{1}{2}$
6.00	4	1.75	$2\frac{1}{2}$
5.50	5	1.50	$3\frac{1}{2}$
5.00	6	1.25	$4\frac{1}{2}$
4.50	7	1.00	$5\frac{1}{2}$
4.00	8	0.75	$6\frac{1}{2}$
3.50	9	0.60	7
3.00	10		
2.50	12		
2.00	14		

Crochet Abbreviations

alt	alternate(ly)	**dtr**	double treble	**rep**	repeat
approx	approximate(ly)	**foll**	follow(ing)	**RS**	right side of work
beg	begin(ning)	**gr**	group(s)	**ss**	slip stitch in crochet
ch	chain(s)	**grm**	gramme(s)	**sl st**	slip stitch in seaming
cl	cluster(s)	**htr**	half treble	**st(s)**	stitch(es)
cm	centimetre(s)	**in**	inch(es)	**tog**	together
cont	continu(e) (ing)	**inc**	increase	**tr**	treble
dec	decrease	**ISR**	International size range of hooks	**tr tr**	triple treble
dc	double crochet	**No.**	number	**WS**	wrong side of work
		patt	pattern	**yrh**	yarn round hook
		rem	remain(ing)		

SYMBOLS
An asterisk, (*), given in a pattern row denotes that the stitches shown after this sign must be repeated from that point.

Square brackets, [ ], denotes instructions for larger sizes in the pattern.
Round brackets, ( ), denote that this section of the pattern is to be worked for all sizes.

Tension—this is the most important factor in successful crochet. Unless you obtain the tension given for each design, you will not obtain satisfactory results.

Know your yarns
'Yarn' is the word used to describe any spun thread, fine or thick, in natural fibres such as wool, cotton, linen, silk, or in man-made fibres such as Acrilan, Orlon, Nylon or Courtelle.
The word 'ply' indicates the number of spun single threads which have been twisted together to produce a specific yarn. Each single thread may be spun to any thickness so that reference to the ply does not necessarily determine the thickness of the finished yarn, although the terms 2 ply, 3 ply and 4 ply are often used to mean yarns of a recognized thickness.
The following ply classification is broadly applicable to the majority of hand-knitting yarns, whether made from natural fibres, man-made fibres or a blend of both.
Baby yarns are usually made from the highest quality yarns and are available in 2, 3 and 4 ply, also double knitting weights. Baby Quicker-knit yarns are equivalent to a 4 ply but because they are very softly twisted, they are light in weight.
2, 3 and 4 ply yarns are available in natural fibres, man-made fibres, or a blend of both, usually made by twisting two spun single threads together—but there are exceptions to this.
Double knitting yarns are usually made from four spun single threads—although there are exceptions to this—twisted together to produce hard-wearing yarns, virtually double the thickness of 4 ply yarns.
Chunky and double double knitting yarns are extra thick yarns which are ideal for heavier, outdoor garments such as children's anoraks.

Some of these yarns are oiled to give greater warmth and protection.
Crepe yarns are usually available in 4 ply qualities—sometimes called 'single crepe'—and double knitting qualities—called 'double crepe'. They are more tightly twisted than normal yarns and produce a smooth, firm fabric which is particularly hard-wearing.

Very important

Since there is no official standardization, yarns marketed by various Spinners often vary in thickness and yardage. As most yarns are marketed by weight, rather than yardage, even the density of dye used to produce certain colours in each range can result in more or less yarn in each ball, although the structure of the yarn is exactly the same.

If it is impossible to obtain the correct yarn quoted in the instructions, another comparable yarn may be used, provided the same tension as given in the pattern is achieved. The Great Yarn Chart shows equivalent yarns which will work up to the appropriate tension, but it is still essential to work a tension sample before beginning any design.

Always buy sufficient yarn at one time to ensure that all the yarn used is from the same dye lot. Yarn from a different dye lot may vary slightly in colour.

Yarns and metrication

When purchasing yarns, it is advisable to check on the weight of each ball, as they now vary considerably due to the introduction of the metric system. Although this system has already been adopted by most of the Spinners, large stocks of yarn in standard ounces will take some time to run out, so this confused situation will be with us for some time.

Here is a conversion table, giving comparable weights in ounces and grams.

Measurements and metrication

Conversion from Imperial measurements in inches and yards to centimetres and metres is already taking place. To assist the reader, all measurements in these chapters will be given first in metric sizes, followed by comparable Imperial sizes. A conversion chart, showing sizes in centimetres and inches is given on page 64.

Success depends on tension

To make any design successfully it is essential to obtain the correct tension stated in the pattern. This means that the same number of stitches and rows to the centimetre/inch—as originally obtained by the designer—must be achieved.

As a beginner, it is vital to keep on practising and trying to obtain the correct tension. If it is impossible to hold both the yarn and hook comfortably and at the same time obtain the correct tension, then change the hook size. If there are too many stitches to the centimetre/inch, try using one size larger hook; if there are too few stitches to the centimetre/inch, try using one size smaller hook. Too many stitches to the centimetre/inch means that the tension is too tight and too few stitches means that the tension is too loose.

This advice applies not only to the beginner but to all crochet workers beginning a new design. It is so often overlooked on the assumption that the reader's tension is average and therefore accurate. The point to stress is that although all patterns are carefully checked, the original designer of the garment may have produced a slightly tighter, or looser tension than average and all the measurements of the garment will have been based on calculations obtained from this original tension.

Always test that the correct tension is being achieved by working at least a 10.0cm (4in) square. A few minutes spent on this preparation lays the successful foundation for any garment. If it is overlooked, a great deal of work may be undertaken before the error in size is realized. Even half a stitch too many or too few can result in the completed garment being 5.0cm (2in) too large or too small.

Once a tension sample has ben worked, lay it on a flat surface and pin it down. Place a firm rule on the sample and mark out 5.0cm (2in) with pins. Count the number of stitches between the pins very carefully, then check the number of rows to 5.0cm (2in) in the same way.

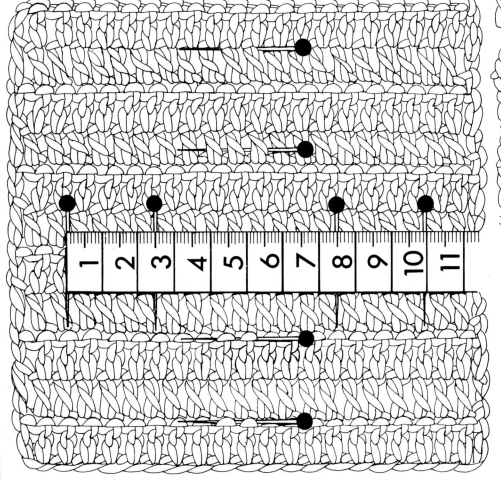

Opposite: This charming crochet purse is of late nineteenth century Irish origin. The delicate Irish lace crochet is backed with pure white silk and the tasseled cord is worked in tubular crochet.

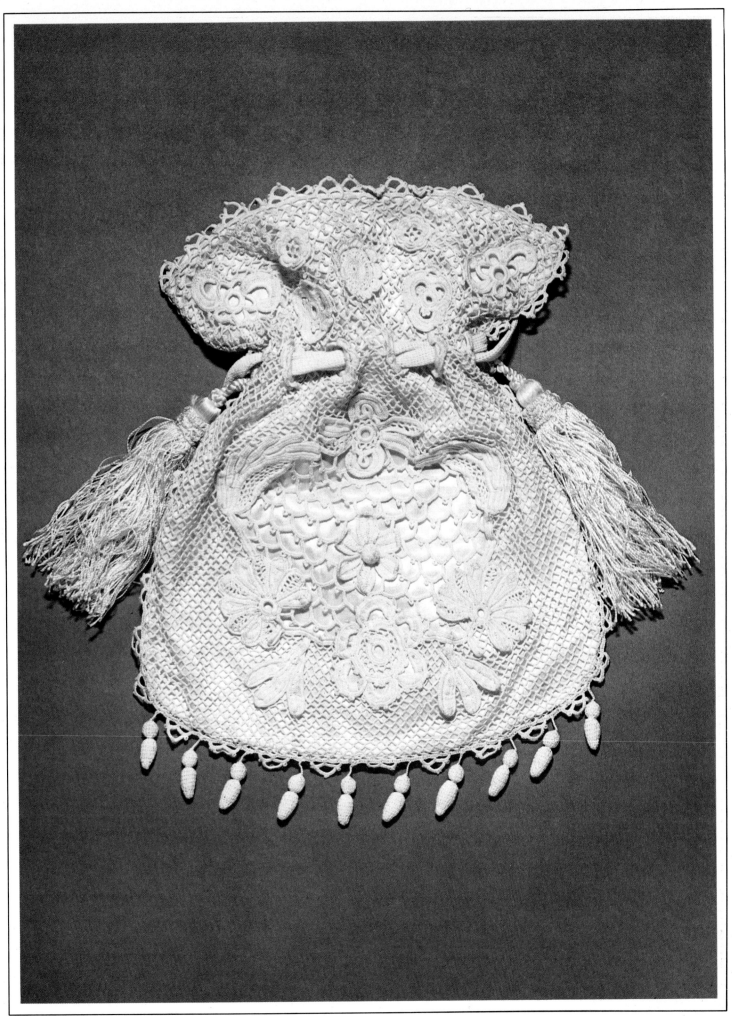

The basic steps

All crochet begins with a slip loop, just as in knitting. The stitches are worked by simply pulling one loop through another and however complicated a stitch may appear, it is merely a variation of this method, always finishing with one loop left on the hook once the stitch has been completed. This loop is a working loop only and is not counted as a stitch. It is the last loop to be fastened off at the end of the crochet, by breaking off the yarn, drawing it through the last loop then pulling this end up tightly.

Holding yarn and hook
Loop the end of a ball of yarn over the index and second finger of the left hand, then under the third finger and round the little finger. Hold the hook in your right hand in the same way as a pen or pencil, gripping the shank firmly between the thumb and forefinger and resting the hooked end against the tip of the second finger.

To make a slip loop
Hold the end of a ball of yarn between the thumb and forefinger of the left hand, using the right hand form a loop and hold this in position with the left hand, allowing the long end of the yarn to stay at the back of the loop. Hold the crochet hook in your right hand, insert the hook

through the loop from the front, catch the long end of the yarn in the hook and pull this loop through, allowing it to stay on the hook. Pull the long end of yarn downwards to tighten the loop.

How to begin
Before you can begin to crochet you must first make a length of loops, or chain stitches, which form a foundation row just as casting on does in knitting.

To make chain stitches.
Hold the hook with the slip loop just made in the right hand and the yarn in the left hand. Pass the hook under, then over the top of the yarn in your left hand, abbreviated as 'yrh', catching the yarn in the curve of the hook. Hold the knot of the slip loop firmly down between the thumb and forefinger of the left hand, then draw the yarn through the loop on the hook from the back to the front. One chain has been made, abbreviated as 'ch', and one working loop is left on the hook. Repeat this action into the chain just made until you have the required length, taking care to move your thumb and forefinger up the chain to hold the stitch you have just made very firmly and allowing the yarn to flow freely over the fingers of the left hand.

Turning chains
Before beginning to work any crochet stitches, it is important to realize the significance of turning chains and the part they play in forming the fabric. Because of the depth of most crochet stitches, it is necessary to add extra chains at the beginning of each row to bring the hook up level with the stitch being used for this row. These are called turning chains, abbreviated as 'turning ch', and the number varies depending on the stitch being worked. They form the first stitch of every row and to compensate for this, the first stitch of every row must be missed and the actual pattern stitch must be worked into the second stitch of the previous row. At the end of each row, the last stitch is then worked into the turning chain of the previous row. Turning chains give a neat, firm edge to the work and unless otherwise stated in a pattern, they form the first stitch, whether working in rows or rounds. Throughout these chapters, the turning chain will be given at the beginning of the row, although some patterns give instructions for working them at the end of the row before turning the work—the important point to remember is that they count as the first stitch of the row. The following table is a guide to the number of turning chains required to give the

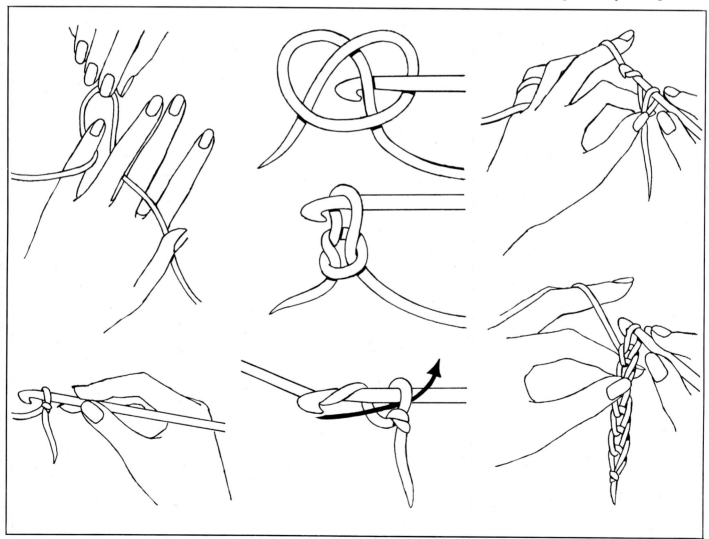

right depth for the stitch being worked:

Double crochet —1 or 2 turning chains
Half treble —2 turning chains
Treble —3 turning chains
Double treble —4 turning chains
Triple treble —5 turning chains

Basic stitches

To work a slip stitch, abbreviated as 'ss'.
Make the required number of ch. *Insert the hook from front to back into the second ch from the hook, yrh and draw loop through both the ch and loop on hook, (one ss has been made), repeat from * into each ch to end.

To work a double crochet, abbreviated as 'dc'.
Make the required number of ch plus one extra ch, i.e., 11ch for 10dc.
1st row Insert the hook from front to back into the 3rd ch from hook, *yrh and draw a loop, through (2 loops on hook), yrh and draw through both loops on hook, (1dc has been made with the 2 missed ch counting as the turning ch), insert the hook from front to back into the next ch and repeat from * into each ch to end. Turn the work so that the last stitch of the row becomes the first stitch of the next row.
2nd row 1ch to count as first dc, miss first dc, *insert the hook from front to back under both loops at the top of the next dc, yrh and draw a loop through, (2 loops on hook), yrh and draw through both loops on hook, repeat from * into every dc, working last dc into turning ch at end of row. Turn.
Repeat the 2nd row for the required length. Fasten off.

To work a half treble, abbreviated as 'htr'.
Make the required number of ch plus one extra ch, i.e., 11ch for 10htr.
1st row Yrh, insert the hook from front to back into the 3rd ch from hook, *yrh and draw a loop through, (3 loops on hook), yrh and draw through all 3 loops on hook, (1htr has been made with the 2 missed ch counting as the turning ch), yrh, insert hook from front to back into the next ch and repeat from * into each ch to end. Turn the work so that the last stitch of the row becomes the first stitch of the next row.
2nd row 2ch to count as first htr, miss first htr, *yrh, insert the hook from front to back under both loops at the top of the next htr, yrh and draw a loop through, (3 loops on hook), yrh and draw through all 3 loops on hook, repeat from * into every htr, working last htr into turning ch at end of row. Turn.
Repeat the 2nd row for the required length. Fasten off.

To work a treble, abbreviated as 'tr'.
Make the required number of ch plus 2 extra ch, i.e., 12ch for 10tr.
1st row Yrh, insert the hook from front to back into the 4th ch from hook, *yrh and draw a loop through, (3 loops on hook), yrh and draw through 2 loops on hook, (2 loops on hook), yrh and draw through 2 loops on hook, (1tr has been made with the 3 missed ch counting as the turning ch), yrh, insert the hook from front to back into the next ch and repeat from * into each ch to end. Turn the work so that the last stitch of the row becomes the first stitch of the next row.
2nd row 3ch to count as first tr, miss first tr, *yrh, insert the hook from front to back under both loops at the top of the next tr, yrh and draw a loop through, (3 loops on hook), yrh and draw through 2 loops on hook, (2 loops on hook), yrh and draw through 2 loops on hook, repeat from * into every tr, working last tr into turning ch at end of row. Turn.
Repeat the 2nd row for the required length. Fasten off.

Slip stitch

Double crochet

Half treble

Treble

Shaping up to crochet

Shaping in crochet is achieved by means of increasing the number of stitches in a row to make the fabric wider, or decreasing the number of stitches in a row to make the fabric narrower. Various methods are used, either by working one more or less stitch at each end of a row, or in the course of a row, by means of additional chains to increase the width, or slipped stitches to decrease the width. Because of the depth of most crochet stitches, unless the shaping is worked very neatly an unsightly gap will be left in the fabric, spoiling the appearance of the completed garment.

How to increase

To increase one stitch at each end of a row
Work the required turning chain, then instead of missing the first stitch, work into this stitch to increase one stitch at the beginning of the row. At the end of the row, work 2 stitches into the turning chain instead of one.

To increase one stitch in the middle of a row
Work in pattern until the position for the increase is reached, work 2 stitches instead of one in to the next stitch, then continue in pattern to the end of the row.

To increase several stitches at the beginning of a row
Before beginning to work in pattern, make a chain equivalent to one less than the extra number of stitches required plus the correct number of turning chains for the stitch being worked. As an example. if 6 stitches are to be increased when working in treble, make 5 extra chain plus 3 turning chain, making a total of 8 in all. Work the next treble for the new row into the 4th chain from the hook, then work 1 treble into each of next 4 chain. Continue working in treble across the row, noting that the position of the turning chain is now at the beginning of the increased stitches.

To increase several stitches at the end of a row

This can be worked in two ways. The first method is to make a separate length of chain in the correct yarn for the exact number of stitches required and join with a slip stitch to the top of the first stitch of the last row, break off the yarn and fasten off and leave for the time being. Work in pattern to the end of the row where the increased stitches are required, then work one stitch into each of the separate length of chain.

The second method is to make provision for these extra stitches at the beginning of the previous row. As an example, if 6 stitches are to be increased at the end of the next row when working in treble, make 10 chain at the beginning of the previous row, miss first chain, work one slip stitch into each of the next 6 chain and leave the other 3 for the first treble of the row, then work in treble to the end of the row. Turn and work back in treble to the 6 slipped stitches, then work one treble into each slip stitch.

How to decrease

To decrease one double crochet at each end of a row

Make 1 turning ch and miss the first double crochet, insert hook into next stitch and draw loop through, insert hook into next stitch and draw loop through, (3 loops on hook), yrh and draw through all loops on hook—called dec 1—, work one double crochet into each double crochet until 2 double crochet and the turning chain of the previous row remain, dec 1 as at the beginning of the row, work the last double crochet into the turning chain.

To decrease one half treble at each end of a row

Make 2 turning chain and miss the first half treble, yrh, insert hook into next stitch and draw loop through, insert hook into next stitch and draw loop through, (4 loops on hook), yrh and draw through all loops on hook—called dec 1—, work one half treble into each half treble until 2 half treble and the turning chain of the previous row remain, dec 1 as at the beginning of the row, work the last half treble into the turning chain.

To decrease one treble at each end of a row

Make 3 turning chain and miss the first treble, yrh, insert hook into the next stitch and draw loop through, yrh and draw through 2 loops on hook, yrh, insert hook into next stitch and draw loop through, yrh and draw through 2 loops on hook, (3 loops on hook), yrh and draw through all loops on hook—called dec 1—, work one treble into each treble until 2 treble and the turning chain of the previous row remain, dec 1 as at the beginning of the row, work the last treble into the turning chain.

To decrease one stitch in the middle of a row

Work in pattern until the position for the decrease is reached, then dec 1 over the next 2 stitches as given for decreasing at each end of a row, and continue in pattern to the end of a row.

To decrease several stitches at the beginning of a row

Slip stitch over the required number of stitches to be decreased and into the next stitch, work the required number of turning chains to form the first stitch, then continue in pattern to the end.

To decrease several stitches at the end of a row

Work in pattern along the row until the required number of stitches to be decreased remain, noting that the turning chain of the previous row must be counted as one of the stitches, then turn the work and leave these stitches unworked.

Helpful hints!

When increasing or decreasing in the middle of a row, mark the position where the shaping is to be worked with a length of coloured thread.

To work a double increase, follow the same instructions but work 3 stitches instead of 2 into the foundation stitch.

To work a double decrease, follow the same instructions but work across 3 stitches instead of 2 before completing the decreasing.

Crochet in rounds

The word 'round' refers to the working method, where the work is not turned at the end as when working in rows but is continued round and round to form a flat, or tubular fabric, joining the last stitch of each round to the first.

When this method is used to produce a flat fabric, an infinite variety of shapes may be formed which may be used as large, separate motifs, or a number of smaller motifs which may then be joined together to form cushions, afghans or blankets and even garments. Each motif may be worked in one single colour, or each round in a different colour to produce a multi-coloured, patchwork effect. Providing the same thickness of yarn is used throughout, it is an ideal way of using up oddments of yarn to make colourful and economical pram and cot blankets.

Where the method of working in rounds is used to produce a tubular fabric, it has the same effect as knitting in rounds to make a fabric without seams.

To work a flat fabric in rounds
To keep the fabric flat, it must begin with a small number of stitches, which are then increased on every round until the required diameter is achieved. This shaping can be achieved either by means of additional stitches or chain spaces.

To make a circular motif
Begin by making 4 chain to form the centre of the motif. Loop the chain round to form a circle and join the last chain to the first chain by means of a slip stitch. Into this circle work twice the number of stitches of the original chain, using the required number of chain to form the first stitch and joining the last stitch to the top of the turning chain with a slip stitch. 8 stitches. On the next round, work the turning chain to count as the first stitch, then work one stitch into the same place as the base of the turning chain and continue working 2 stitches into each stitch to the end, joining as before. 16 stitches. On each subsequent round, increase a total of 8 stitches by increasing in the first and every alternate stitch in the next round; in the first and every following 3rd stitch in the next round; in the first and every following 4th stitch in the next round, then continue in this way depending on the size of motif required.

To make a square motif
Make the centre circle as given for the circular motif, having about 6 chain. If only one colour is being used, each round can be worked without having to break off the yarn.

1st round 3ch to count as first tr, 2tr into circle, 2ch, (3tr into circle, 2ch) 3 times. Join with a ss to 3rd of first 3ch.

2nd round 2ch, (3tr, 2ch, 3tr) into first 2ch space to form corner, *1ch, (3tr, 2ch, 3tr) into next 2ch sp, rep from * twice more. Join with a ss to first of first 2ch.

3rd round 3ch to count as first tr, 2tr into first ch space beyond ss join of previous round, 1ch, *(3tr, 2ch, 3tr) into corner 2ch space, 1ch, 3tr into next 1ch space, 1ch, rep from * twice more, (3tr, 2ch, 3tr) into last 2ch space, 1ch. Join with a ss to 3rd of first 3ch.

4th round 2ch, 3tr into next 1ch space, 1ch, *(3tr, 2ch, 3tr) into corner 2ch space, 1ch, (3tr into next 1ch space, 1ch) twice, rep from * twice more, (3tr, 2ch, 3tr) into last 2ch space, 1ch, 3tr into last 1ch space. Join with a ss to first of first 2ch. Fasten off.

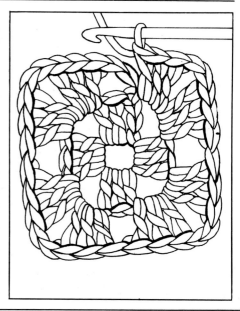

If a separate colour is being used for each round, each colour must be broken off at the end of the round. Each colour for this motif is coded as A, B, C and D.
Using A, make the centre circle and work the 1st round as given for the square motif. Break off A.

2nd round Join in B to any 2ch space with a ss, 3ch to count as first tr, 2tr into same ch space, *1ch, 3tr, 2ch and 3tr into next 2ch space to form corner, rep from * twice more, 1ch, 3tr into same ch space as beg of round, 2ch. Join with a ss to 3rd of first 3ch. Break off B.

3rd round Join in C to any 2ch space with a ss, 3ch to count as first tr, 2tr into same ch space, *1ch, 3tr into next 1ch space, 1ch, 3tr, 2ch and 3tr into corner 2ch space, rep from * twice more, 1ch, 3tr into next 1ch space, 1ch, 3tr into same ch space as beg of round, 2ch. Join with a ss to 3rd of first 3ch. Break off C.

4th round Join in D to any 2ch space with a ss, 3ch to count as first tr, 2tr into same ch space, *1ch, (3tr into next 1ch space, 1ch) twice, 3tr, 2ch and 3tr into corner 2ch space, rep from * twice more, 1ch, 3tr into next 1ch space, 1ch, 3tr into next 1ch space, 1ch, 3tr into same ch space as beg of round, 2ch. Join with a ss to 3rd of first 3ch. Fasten off.

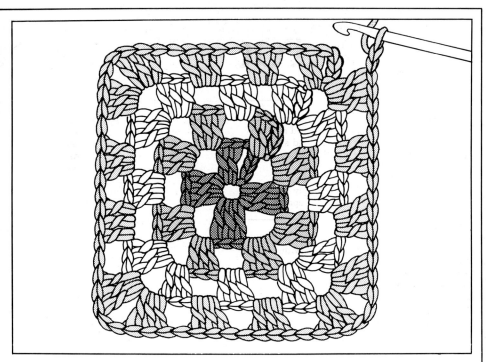

To work a tubular fabric in rounds
The fabric must begin with the required number of chains to give the total circumference of the item being made. Because the right side of the work is always facing you, even basic stitches, such as trebles, will have a different appearance. If the work is to be divided at any point and continued in rows, this difference in appearance must be taken into account at the onset. In this case, each round will be joined to the first stitch but the work will then be turned, just as when working in rows, and continued along the reversed side of the fabric.

To work tubular fabric without turning
Make the required number of chains and join the last chain to the first by means of a slip stitch, taking care to see that the length of chain does not become twisted. Work the required number of turning chains to form the first stitch and miss the first chain, then work one stitch into each chain to end. Join the last stitch to the top of the turning chain with a slip stitch. Continue in this way for the required length, then fasten off.

To work tubular fabric turning each round
Make the required number of chains and work the first round as given for tubular fabric without turning. After joining the round with a slip stitch, turn the work so that the other side of the fabric is facing you, make the required number of turning chains and miss the first stitch, then continue in pattern to the end of the round, joining with a slip stitch as before. Continue in this way for the required length, or until the point where the work is to be divided is reached, then continue working in rows, without joining.

Finishing touches

The making up of a garment and any additional finishing touches can make or mar the final results. It is essential to pay attention to the correct handling of the yarn which has been used, to the best methods of seaming the finished sections and to the way of making, or applying any individual trimmings.

Handling yarns
Each yarn, whether it is made from natural or man-made fibres, requires a different method of handling in making up and after care. The Home Laundering Consultative Council has compiled a washing, ironing and dry-cleaning code in respect of hand knitting yarns and the relative symbols are shown on most ball bands. Read these instructions very carefully before attempting to press any of the sections. If you have not used the correct yarn given in the instructions, check and make absolutely sure that the substitute you have chosen needs pressing, regardless of what instructions are given in the making up section of the pattern.

	HOT	WARM	COOL	DO NOT IRON
IRONING				
DRYCLEAN	(A)	(P)	(F)	⊗
	Usual dry cleaning	Normally drycleanable in most solvents. If drycleaned inform cleaner of composition of yarn.	Drycleanable in some solvents It is important that the cleaner is informed of the composition of the yarn if dry-cleaning is to be undertaken.	DO NOT DRYCLEAN

Blocking and pressing

As so many of the yarns now available do not require pressing, it is not always necessary to block out each section to the correct size and shape. However, any crochet stitch which is very open in texture will benefit if it is blocked out, then covered with a damp cloth and left until the cloth is absolutely dry.

If pressing is advised, place each section right side down on an ironing pad and pin it evenly round the edges to the pad. Once the piece is pinned out, making sure that it is not stretched and that the stitches and rows run in straight lines, check with a rule that the width and length are the same as those given in the instructions. Using a clean damp, or dry cloth and a warm or cool iron, as given in the instructions, press the piece evenly, putting the iron down and lifting it up again without moving it across the surface of the cloth. Allow the piece to cool before removing the pins.

Seaming

Crochet sections may be joined together either by means of a blunt ended sewing needle threaded with the same yarn, or by means of a crochet hook and double crochet. The choice of seaming will depend on the finished article but the double crochet method gives a very firm edge, which can look most effective when it is worked on the right side of the item, giving added interest to the fabric.

Back stitch seam

Using a blunt ended needle threaded with yarn, begin by working two or more small stitches, one on top of the other, to secure the yarn, *with the needle at the back of the work, move approximately 0.5cm (¼in) along the seam to the left, insert the needle through to the front of the work then take it back along to the right and insert it into the end of the previous stitch, repeat from * to the end of the seam. Fasten off securely.

Oversewn seam

Using a blunt ended needle threaded with yarn, secure the yarn as given for back stitch seam, *pass the needle over the top of the two edges, through from the back to the front and pull the yarn through, repeat from * to the end of the seam. Fasten off securely.

Double crochet seam

Insert the crochet hook from front to back through the edge stitch of both pieces to be joined, put the yarn round the hook and pull loop through, then complete one double crochet in the usual way, insert the hook approximately 0.5cm (¼in) along to the left from the last double crochet and work another double crochet. Continue in this way until the seam is completed, then fasten off.

Finishing touches
Casing or herringbone stitch

This method is used to finish the waist of a skirt or trousers. Cut the elastic to the size required and join into a circle. Mark off the waistband and elastic into quarters, then pin the elastic into position on the wrong side of the work. Taking care to distribute the crochet evenly, hold the waistband over the fingers of the left hand. Thread a blunt ended needle and secure the yarn to the fabric. Take the yarn over the elastic and insert the sewing needle lightly through the fabric from right to left, draw the yarn through, take the yarn back over the elastic to the top edge about two stitches along, insert the sewing needle lightly through the fabric from right to left again and draw the yarn through. Continue in this way all round the waistband. Fasten off securely.

Picking up stitches

This method is widely used for finishing neckbands and borders. Have the right side of the work facing and join in the yarn with a slip stitch. Keeping the yarn at the back of the work, insert the crochet hook through the edge from front to back, pull the yarn through and complete the stitch as given in the instructions. To ensure that stitches are picked up evenly and are well spaced, mark each section with pins at regular intervals and pick up the same number of stitches between the pins.

Twisted cords

The number of strands of yarn required will vary according to the thickness of the cord and the yarn being used. Take the required number of stands and cut them into lengths 3 times the length of the finished cord. Enlist the aid of another person, each one taking one end of the strands and knotting them together, then insert a pencil into each knot. Each person should twist the strands to the right until they are tightly twisted. Holding the strands taut, fold them in half at the centre and knot the 2 ends together. Holding the knot, give the cord a sharp shake, then smooth it from the knot to the folded end to even out the twists. Make another knot at the folded end, cut through the folded loops and tease out the ends.

needle threaded with yarn, insert the needle at one edge of the card and under the strands, taking them all together, then fasten off securely. Cut through the strands of yarn at the other untied edge of the card. Finish the tassel by winding an end of yarn several times round the top folded ends and fasten off securely, leaving an end long enough to sew the tassel to the garment.

Pompons

Cut 2 circles of cardboard to the size required for the finished pompon, then cut a circle from the centre of each. Place the 2 pieces of card together and wind the yarn evenly round until the centre hole is nearly filled, then thread the yarn into a blunt ended sewing needle to completely fill the centre. Cut through the yarn round the outer edge, working between the 2 pieces of card. Take a piece of yarn and tie very securely round the centre of the pompon and between the 2 pieces of card, leaving an end long enough to sew the pompon to the garment. Cut away the card and trim pompon to shape.

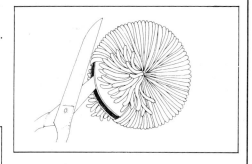

Threading beads or sequins on to yarn

To thread beads or sequins on to a ball of yarn before beginning to work with it, fold a length of sewing cotton in half and thread a fine sewing needle with both cut ends, leaving a loop of cotton. Pass the end of the ball of yarn to be used through the loop of cotton and slide beads or sequins on to the needle, down the cotton and on to the yarn.

Tassels

Cut a piece of cardboard the width of the required length of the tassel. Wind the yarn round and round the card until the desired thickness is obtained. Using a blunt ended

Buttonholes & buttons

Neat buttonholes, either horizontal or vertical, can easily be worked in one with the main fabric or incorporated into a separate band. Chain button loops are simple to work and are ideal for use on baby garments and frog fastenings add an original touch to any basic garment.

Horizontal buttonholes
Work until the position for the buttonhole is reached. Where this is required as part of the main fabric, finish at the centre front edge before working the buttonhole row. On the next row, work a few stitches to where the buttonhole is required, work two or more chains to take the size of the button being used, miss the same number of stitches in the row below, then pattern to the end of the row. On the next row, work in pattern over the chains in the previous row to complete the buttonhole.

Vertical buttonholes
When using short stitches, such as double crochet or half treble, work until the position for the buttonhole is reached. On the next row work a few stitches to where the buttonhole is required, turn, then work the required number of rows over these stitches to take the size of button being used, ending at the inner edge. Work in slip stitch down the inner edge of the rows just worked to the last complete row worked and pattern to the end of this row. Work across these remaining stitches for the same number of rows as the first side, then continue across all the stitches to complete the buttonhole. When a longer stitch, such as treble, is being used, work as given for vertical buttonhole ending at front edge. Do not break off yarn. Using a separate length of yarn, begin at inner edge of buttonhole and complete second side to match first side. Break off yarn. Return to the original yarn and continue across all the stitches to complete the buttonhole.

Button loops
These should be worked on the last row of any edge where buttonholes are required. Work the edging as given in the instructions until the last row is reached. Mark the position of the buttons on the edging, then continue in pattern for the last row, making button loops as the markers are reached by working two or more chains to take the size of button being used, miss the same number of stitches in the row below, then continue in pattern to the next marker. Make the required number of loops in the same way.

Frog fastening
The size and thickness of the fastening will depend on the type of garment being trimmed. As an example, use a No.5.00 (ISR) crochet hook and 3 strands of double knitting yarn to make approximately 80ch. Fasten off and darn in the ends. Twist into shape and sew together, as shown.

Buttons

It is often very difficult to find buttons which exactly match the yarn used for a garment, or the correct size of button required. Crochet covered buttons are simple to work and provide an inexpensive way of adding individual touches to any garment.

Lilac button

Use No.2.50 (ISR) hook and 4 ply yarn. Make 3ch. Join with a ss to first ch to form circle.
1st round 2ch to count as first htr, 7htr into circle. Join with a ss to 2nd of first 3ch. 8 sts.
2nd round 2ch to count as first htr, working in to back loop only of each st, work 1htr into base of first 2ch, 2htr into each htr to end. Join with a ss to 2nd of first 2ch. 16 sts.
3rd round 2ch, 1htr into back loop only of each htr to end. Join with a ss to 2nd of first 2ch.
4th round As 3rd.
5th round 1ch to count as first dc, *miss 1htr, 1dc into each of next 2htr, rep from * to end. Join with a ss to first ch. 11 sts.
6th round 1ch, *1dc into next dc, miss 1dc, rep from * to end. Join with a ss to first ch. 6sts.
Complete as given for small blue button.

Gold button

Use No.3.00 (ISR) hook and glitter yarn. Make 2ch. Into first of these 2ch work 8dc, do not join. Into each dc work 2htr. Join with a ss to first htr.
Break off yarn, thread through each st round edge, draw up and fasten off securely.

Pink button worked spirally

Use No.3.00 (ISR) hook and double knitting yarn. Make 2ch. Into first of these 2ch work 8dc, do not join. Cont working in rounds without joining, work (2dc into next dc, 1dc into next dc) 12 times, (there will now be 20 sts in round), or until work is required size.
Next round Work 1dc into each dc all round, do not join.
Next round (dec round) (Miss 1dc, 1dc into next dc) 10 times, do not join.
Insert cotton wool or button mould into cover and cont to dec in this way until hole is filled. Fasten off.

Yellow button with petals

This requires a button mould 2.5cm (*1in*) diameter with 2 or 4 holes in it. Use No.2.50 (ISR) hook and 4 ply yarn. Make 3ch. Join with a ss to first ch to form circle.
1st round 1ch, 8dc into circle. Join with a ss to first ch. 9 sts.
2nd round 1ch, 1dc into same place, 2dc into each dc to end. Join with a ss to first ch. 18 sts.
3rd round 1ch, 1dc into each dc to end. Join with a ss to first ch.
4th round As 3rd.
5th and 6th rounds As given for small blue button.
Complete as given for small blue button.
Petals
Make 3ch. Join with a ss to first ch to form circle. Into circle work (1dc, 2tr, 1dc) 5 times. Join with a ss to first dc. Fasten off.
Centre
Leaving a long end make 2ch. Into the first of these 2ch work (yrh, insert hook into ch and draw a loop through, drawing it up to 1.5cm (*½in*)) 3 times, yrh and draw through all 7 loops on hook, 1ch. Fasten off leaving a long end of yarn.
Sew petals to top of button. Thread 2 ends of centre through the holes of button, pull up tightly and fasten off at back.

Ring button

This requires a ring 2.5cm (*1in*) diameter. Use No.3.00 (ISR) hook and double knitting yarn. Using first colour, make 3ch. Join with a ss to first ch to form circle.
1st round 1ch, 11dc into circle. Join with a ss to first ch. 12 sts. Break off yarn.
2nd round Join in 2nd colour, 1ch, hold the ring behind the work, then working over the ring make 1dc into base of 1ch, 2dc into each dc to end. Join with a ss to first ch. Fasten off.

Small blue button

Use No.2.50 (ISR) hook and 4 ply yarn. Make 3ch. Join with a ss to first ch to form circle.
1st round 1ch, 5dc into circle. Join with a ss to first ch. 6 sts.
2nd round 1ch, 1dc into same place, 2dc into each dc to end. Join with a ss to first ch. 12 sts.
3rd round 1ch, 2dc into next dc, *1dc into next dc, 2dc into next dc, rep from * to end. Join with a ss to first ch. 18 sts.
4th round 1ch, 1dc into each dc to end. Join with a ss to first ch.
5th round 1ch, 1dc into next dc, *miss 1dc, 1dc into each of next 2dc, rep from * to last dc, miss last dc. Join with a ss to first ch. 12 sts.
6th round 1ch, *miss 1dc, 1dc into next dc, rep from * to last dc, miss last dc. Join with a ss to first ch. 6 sts.
Break off yarn leaving an end long enough to sew on button. Insert button mould into cover, thread yarn through rem sts, draw up and fasten off securely.

Light green button

Work as given for small blue button but turn cover inside out before inserting button mould.

Two-colour blue button

Work as given for small blue button, working first 3 rounds in one colour and remaining rounds in 2nd colour.

Dark green button

Use No.2.50 (ISR) hook and 4 ply yarn. Make 3ch. Join with a ss to first ch to form circle.
1st round 1ch, 7dc into circle. Join with a ss to first ch. 8 sts.
2nd round 3ch to count as first tr, 1tr back into 8th dc of last round, 1tr into next dc beyond the 3ch, 1tr into base of 3ch, *1tr into next dc of last round, 1tr back into previous dc, rep from * to end. Join with ss to 3rd of first 3ch.
3rd round Ss into sp between 2tr, 1ch to count as first dc, 1dc into same place, 1dc between next 2tr, *2dc between next 2tr (i.e. into the sp between the 2 crossed tr), 1dc between next 2tr (i.e., between the pairs of crossed tr), rep from * to end. Join with a ss to first ch.
4th round 1ch to count as first dc, miss 1dc, *1dc into next dc, miss 1dc, rep from * to end. Join with a ss to first ch.
5th round As 4th.
Complete as given for small blue button.

Edgings & braids

Crochet edgings and braids can either be applied directly to the main fabric, or worked as a separate strip and then sewn to the fabric. They can be thick of fine, depending on the type of yarn being used—bold and wide multi-coloured bands or narrow and delicate strips of lace. Their uses are almost too numerous to list—edgings for household linens, baby garments and fashion garments, or separate braids worked as hatbands, cushion and curtain trimmings or neat belts.

Edgings

An edging is usually applied directly to the main fabric as a means of neatening openings, such as neckbands, or as an additional decorative trimming.

Crab stitch edging

This is one of the simplest edgings, being worked in double crochet either in rows or rounds. Work along the edge in double crochet and if this is a circular opening, join with a slip stitch to the first stitch. Do not turn the work but work another row or round of double crochet back along the edge already worked, making one double crochet into each double crochet and working from left to right instead of from right to left. Fasten off.

Picot edging

There are many variations of picot edging but this method is simple to work in rows or rounds. Work along the edge in double crochet and if this is a circular opening, join with a slip stitch to the first stitch and turn, making sure that you have a nunber of stitches divisible by 2 plus one. On the next row or round, work 1ch to count as the first dc and miss the first dc ,*1dc into next dc, 3ch, ss into first of these 3ch to form picot, 1dc into next dc, rep from * to end. Fasten off.

Cluster edging

Work along the edge in double crochet, making sure that you have a number of stitches divisible by 2 plus one. Turn.

Next row 2ch to count as first dc and 1ch sp, * miss next dc, (yrh, insert hook into next dc and draw through a loose loop) 4 times into same dc, (9 loops on hook), yrh and draw through all loops on hook, 1ch, rep from * to last 2dc, miss 1dc, 1dc into last dc. Fasten off.

Shell edging.

Work along the edge in double crochet, making sure that you have a number of stitches divisible by 4 plus one. Turn.

Next row 1ch to count as first ss, *miss 1dc, 4tr into next dc, miss 1dc, 1ss into next dc, rep from * to end. Fasten off.

Crab stitch edging

Picot edging

Cluster edging

Shell edging

Separate edgings

These edgings are worked for the required length and then sewn in place to the main fabric.

Picot edging

*Make 3ch, into the first of these 3ch work 2dc, do not turn but repeat from * until the edging is the required length. Fasten off.

Ring picot edging

*Make 5ch, into the first of these 5ch work 1tr, do not turn but repeat from * until the edging is the required length. Fasten off.

Lace ring edging

Each ring is formed and one side worked into before making the next ring then, when the required length has been made, the second side of each ring is completed.

1st row *Make 10ch, remove hook from last ch and insert into first ch, draw loop of last ch through first ch to form ring, work 6dc along one side of ring, rep from * until edging is required length. Do not fasten off.

2nd row *Work 6 more dc into this ring along other side of ch, ss into side of last dc of previous ring, rep from * until each ring has been completed. Join with a ss to first dc. Fasten off.

Braids

These braids may be used as trimmings, or the wider examples can be used to make attractive belts.

Ric rac braid
Make 5ch.
1st row Into 5th ch from hook work 1dc. Turn.
2nd row 4ch, work 1dc into dc of previous row.
Turn.
Repeat the 2nd row for the required length.
Fasten off.
Birds eye braid
Worked in 2 colours, coded as A and B. Using
A, make a number of chain divisible by 3 plus
one, joining in B on last chain. Do not break
off A.
1st row Using B, 1ch to count as first dc, *4ch,
miss 2ch in A, 1dc into next ch, rep from * to
end, work 2 more dc into end ch then rep from
* along the other side of commencing ch, work
1 more dc into the last ch. Break off B.
2nd row With RS of work facing insert hook
from front to back into the last of the commencing ch in A, keeping the hook behind the
row in B draw a loop of A through, 2ch to count
as first htr, working only into the missed sts of
the commencing ch and holding the 4ch loops
in B forward and working behind them, work
1htr into each of next 2ch, *2htr into next ch,
1htr into next ch, rep from * to end, 2ch, ss into
last ch noting that this is the same ch as the last
st in B, 2ch, then cont along other side of work in
same way. Break off A.
3rd row With RS of work facing, rejoin B to
2nd of 2ch at beg of 2nd row, 1ch to count as
first dc, *insert hook under the 4ch loop and
work 1dc into next htr catching the 4ch loop at
the same time, 1dc into each of next 2htr, rep
from * to end, do not turn but work a row of
crab st back along this edge. Fasten off.
Rep 3rd row and crab st along other edge to
complete braid.
Chevron braid
Worked in 2 colours, coded as A and B. Using
A, make a chain the required length, making
sure that you have a number of stitches
divisible by 4 plus 3 and one extra turning
chain.
1st row Using A, into 3rd ch from hook work
1htr, 1htr into each ch to end. Do not break off
A but work 2ch, 1ss into same ch as last htr,
2ch, then continue along other side of commencing ch, working 1htr into each ch to end,
2ch, 1ss into same ch as last htr, 2ch. Join with a
ss to 2nd off first 2ch. Fasten off.
2nd row With RS of work facing join B with a
ss to 2nd of first 2ch, 1ch to count as first dc,
1dc into each of next 2htr, *miss 1htr, insert
hook into space between the 2 rows along
commencing ch and immediately below the next
htr (the htr after the missed htr), yrh and draw
a loop through long enough to reach to the top
of the row being worked, insert hook into the
missed htr, yrh and draw through 2 loops on
hook, yrh and draw through rem 2 loops,
1htr into each of next 3htr, rep from * to end,
2ch, 1ss into end of commencing ch, 2ch, 1ss
into first htr along other side, 1ch to count as
first dc, **1dc into each of next 3htr, insert hook
into same space as first long st on other side,
yrh and draw a long loop through, insert hook
into next htr, yrh and draw through 2 loops on
hook, yrh and draw through rem 2 loops, rep
from ** to last 3htr, 1dc into each of next 3htr,
2ch, 1ss into end of commencing ch, 2ch, 1ss
into 2nd of first 2ch along other side, then
continue along this side.
3rd row *3ch, (yrh, insert hook into same st as
last ss, yrh and draw a loop through, yrh and
draw through 2 loops on hook) twice, yrh and
draw through all 3 loops on hook, miss 3dc, 1ss
in to next dc, rep from * to end, 2ch, 1ss into
end of commencing ch, 2ch, 1ss into first dc
along other side, then rep from * along this side.
Fasten off.

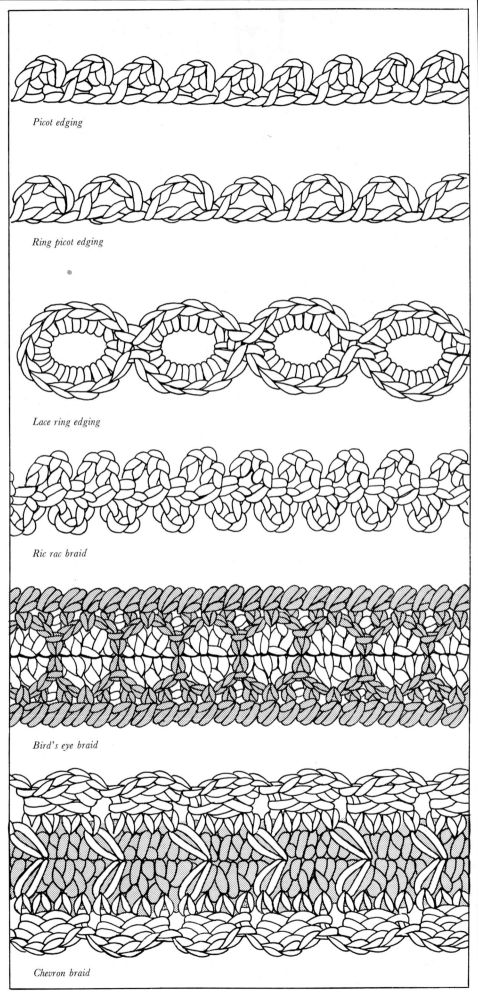

Picot edging

Ring picot edging

Lace ring edging

Ric rac braid

Bird's eye braid

Chevron braid

New ways of shaping

The usual way of shaping, by increasing or decreasing stitches at a given point has already been explained but a far more interesting effect can be achieved by working a section from side edge to side edge and using stitches of different depths, or turning at a given point in a row, to form the shaping. These methods are an ideal way of working a full skirt, a beret, matinee jacket or something as simple as a man's tie. Before beginning to work a section using different stitches, it is essential to ensure that the fabric formed will complement any other sections which may be worked in the normal way. Because they are worked from side edge to side edge, the stitches which form the fabric will lie vertically in rows instead of horizontally. The narrowest part of the section should be worked in double crochet which will form a dense fabric, with half trebles used for the next shaped section and the widest part may then be worked in trebles or a patterned stitch.

Shaping by turning

This method is also worked from side edge to side edge and the shaping is achieved by turning at a given point in a row and leaving the remaining stitches unworked for the time being. Begin by making this simple tie, to see how easily this method of shaping may be worked. You will need 1 x 50 grm ball of a 4 ply yarn, an oddment of contrast colour for the edging and a No.3.00 (ISR) crochet hook. Make 261ch in the usual way.

1st row Into 3rd ch from hook work 1dc, 1dc into each ch to end. Turn.
Work 2 more rows dc.
4th row (shaping row) 1ch, miss first dc, 1dc in to each of next 99sts, 1ss into each of next 10sts, turn.
5th row Ss into each of next 10ss, 1dc into each dc to end. Turn.
6th row 1ch, miss first dc, 1dc into each of next 89dc, 1ss into each of next 10dc, turn.
7th row As 5th.
Rep 4th and 5th rows once more. Work 3 more rows dc across all sts. Fasten off.
Edging Using B and with RS of work facing, work round all edges in dc. Join with a ss to first dc. Fasten off.

Shaping by using different stitches

This method is most effective when it is used to shape a skirt. Before beginning, you must first determine the length of skirt required and the tension which will be achieved using the hook size and yarn selected, over both double crochet and trebles or a patterned stitch. The correct position for the shaping must also be worked out to give a good swing to the skirt. As an example, say the required skirt length is 53.5cm (*21in*) from waist to lower edge, the first position for shaping should occur approximately 7.5cm (*3in*) below the waist and the second position approximately 15.0cm (*6in*) below the waist. For each 7.5cm (*3in*) less in overall length, allow approximately 0.5cm (*¼in*) less to each shaping position, i.e., on a skirt with an overall length of 30.5cm (*12in*), allow 5.5cm (*2¼in*) to the first shaping position and 11.5cm (*4½in*) to the second position.
The pattern given here uses a 4 ply yarn and a No.3.50 (ISR) crochet hook to give a skirt length of 53.5cm (*21in*). Allow 8 x 50 grm balls for a 91.5cm (*36in*) hip size and 1 additional ball for each subsequent size. The correct tension is 20tr and 22dc to 10.0cm (*4in*).
Make 111ch and beg at waist, working from top to lower edge.
1st row (RS) Into 3rd ch from hook work 1dc, 1dc into each of next 14ch, 1htr into each of next 16ch, 1tr into each of next 78ch. Turn. 110 sts.
2nd row 3ch to count as first tr, 1tr into each of next 77tr, 1htr into each of next 16htr, 1dc into each of next 16dc. Turn.
3rd row 1ch to count as first dc, 1dc into each of next 15dc, 1htr into each of next 16htr, 1tr into each tr to end. Turn.
The 2nd and 3rd rows form the pattern and are repeated throughout. Continue in pattern until work measures 68.5cm (*27in*) from beginning, or required length measured across waist edge. Fasten off. Join cast on edge to cast off edge, leaving an opening for a zip fastener. Sew in zip, Sew elastic inside waist edge using casing stitch. Use one of the edgings given earlier to neaten lower edge.

Shaping using turning and different stitches

Both of these methods may be combined to produce a beret, or an interesting fluted sleeve which will give an original touch to an otherwise plain jersey or dress. Here again, the finished depth and the position for the shaping must first be determined. A vertical striped effect can quite easily be obtained by working an even number of rows in two or more colours.
Beret
Make the required number of chain to fit the depth of crown. Work 1 row treble.
2nd row 3ch to count as first tr, miss first tr, 1tr into each tr to last 12 sts, 1dc into each of next 6 sts, turn, leaving rem 6 sts unworked.
3rd row Ss into each of first 6dc, 1tr into each tr to last 6 sts, 1dc into each of next 2 sts, turn.
4th row Ss into each of first 2dc, 1tr into each tr to last 6ss, turn.
5th row Ss into each of first 6sts, 1tr into each st to end. Turn.
Work 2 rows tr across all sts. Repeat from the 2nd row until lower edge fits round head. Fasten off. Join cast on edge to cast off edge. Gather up top of crown. Work 2 rounds dc round lower edge. Fasten off. Trim with pompon.

Fluted sleeve.

The pattern given here uses the same yarn, hook size and tension as given for the skirt, to give a sleeve seam of 12.5cm (*5in*), to fit an armhole on an 86.5cm (*34in*) bust size. Make 22ch and work from side edge to side edge.
1st row (RS) Into 4th ch from hook work 1tr, 1tr into each ch to end. Turn. 20 sts.
2nd row 3ch to count as first tr, 1tr into each tr to end. Turn.
Shape top
Next row 3ch, work 1htr into 3rd of these 3ch from hook to increase 2 sts, 1tr into each tr to end. 22 sts.
Next row 3ch, 1tr into each of next 19tr, 1htr into next htr, 1htr into turning ch. Turn.
Next row 3ch, work 1htr into 3rd of these 3ch to increase 2 sts, 1htr into each of next 2htr, 1tr into each tr to end. Turn. 24 sts.
Next row 3ch, 1tr into each of next 19tr, 1htr into each of next 3htr, 1htr into turning ch. Turn.
Cont inc in this way, rep last 2 rows 4 times more. 32 sts.
Next row 5ch, work 1dc into 3rd of these 5ch, 1dc into each of next 2ch to inc 4 sts, 1htr into each of next 12htr, 1tr into each tr to end. Turn.
Next row 3ch, 1tr into each of next 19tr, 1htr into each of next 12htr, 1dc into each of next 3dc, 1dc into turning ch. Turn.
Cont inc in this way, rep last 2 rows twice more. 44 sts. Work 12 rows patt as now set without shaping, ending at top edge.
Next row Ss across first 4dc and into next dc, 1ch to count as first dc, patt to end. Turn. 40 sts.
Next row Patt to end. Turn.
Rep last 2 rows twice more. 32 sts.
Next row Ss across first 2htr and into next htr, 2ch to count as first htr, patt to end. Turn. 30 sts.
Next row Patt to end. Turn.
Rep last 2 rows until 20tr rem. Work 1 more row tr. Fasten off. Join cast on edge to cast off edge to form underarm seam. Set sleeve into armhole, easing in fullness at shoulder.

Opposite, (l. to r.) : Sections of skirt and beret, the completed tie, and a section of the sleeve showing the shaping using different stitches and turning rows.
Top : the finished skirt, beret and sleeve.

Finished skirt

Finished beret

Finished sleeve

Stripes are so simple

Striped effects are the quickest and simplest way of giving even the most basic stitches a completely different look, or a perfectly plain garment the couture touch. They can be incorporated into an all-over pattern, or used as bands of contrast colours round the welt or cuffs of a jersey. Providing yarns of the same thickness are used, they can be an interesting and economical way of using up oddments.

Horizontal stripes

These may be formed by working 2, 4, 6 or more even number of rows in each colour in turn, carrying the yarn not in use up the side of the work until it is required again. If an odd number of rows is worked for each stripe, care must be taken to ensure that the number of colours used will allow for the yarn to be at the correct end of the work when it is required again, otherwise each colour must be broken off and rejoined again. To bring a new colour into use at the beginning of a row, work the last stitch of the previous row until 2 loops remain on the hook, then draw the new colour through these 2 loops to complete the stitch. Turn the work and continue with the new colour, bringing in each subsequent colour in the same way.

Checked effects can be achieved on a striped background by working vertical rows of chains directly on to the right side of the fabric at regular intervals.

Vertical stripes

These are a little more difficult to work, as the colours must be changed at several points during the course of the same row. When the stripes are narrow, using only 2 or 3 stitches for each colour, it is quite simple to bring in each new colour as it is required, carrying the yarn not in use across the back of the work until it is required again.

For wider stripes, however, it is not advisable to use this method as, apart from the waste of yarn, there is a tendency to carry the yarn across too tightly causing the fabric to pull out of shape. It is much better to divide each colour into small, separate balls before beginning to work and use a separate ball of yarn for each stripe.

One important point to remember is that vertical, or diagonal stripes worked by carrying the yarn across the back of the stitches produce a fabric of double thickness, whilst stripes worked by using separate balls of yarn give a fabric of normal thickness.

Bringing in a new colour for vertical or horizontal stripes

Unless each new colour is brought into use correctly the edge of each stripe will be blurred and out of line. To work these samples, use 2 colours coded as A and B.

Carrying yarn across back of work

On a right side row where the yarn is carried across the back of the work, *work one stitch less than the required number of stitches in A, work the next stitch with A leaving the last 2 loops of the stitch on the hook, pick up B and take it over A then conplete the stitch with B, work one stitch less than the required number of stitches in B, work the next stitch with B leaving the last 2 loops of the stitch on the hook, pick up A and take it over B than complete the

stitch with A, repeat from * to the end of the row bringing in colours as required.

On a wrong side row where the yarn is carried across the front of the work, *work one stitch less than the required number of stitches in A, work the next stitch with A leaving the last 2 loops on the hook, bring A forward to front of work, pick up B and take to back of work then complete stitch with B, work one stitch less than the required number of stitches in B, work the next stitch with B leaving the last 2 loops on hook bring B forward to front of work, pick up A and take to back of work then complete stitch with A, repeat from * to the end of the row bringing in colours as required.

Using separate balls of yarn

On a right side row where the yarn is changed at the back of the work, *work one stitch less than the required number of stitches in A, work the next stitch with A leaving last 2 loops on hook, keeping yarn at back of work twist B to the right under and over A and complete stitch with B, work one stitch less than the required number of stitches in B, work the next stitch with B leaving the last 2 loops on hook, keeping yarn at back of work twist A under and over B and complete stitch with A, repeat from * to the end of the row, bringing in colours as required.

On a wrong side row where the yarn is changed at the front of the work, *work one stitch less than the required number of stitches in A, work the next stitch with A leaving the last 2 loops on hook, keeping A at front of work twist B to the right under and over A and across to the back of the work and complete the stitch with B, work one stitch less than the required number of stitches in B, work the next stitch with B leaving the last 2 loops on hook, keeping B at front of work twist A to the right under and over B and across to the back of the work and complete the stitch with A, repeat from * to the end of the row, bringing in colours as required.

Diagonal stripes

Narrow or wide diagonal stripes are worked in the same way as vertical stripes, either by carrying the yarn across the back of the work or by using separate balls of yarn for each stripe. The diagonal effect is achieved by moving one stitch in each colour to the left or right, as desired. The sample given here shows how to work a narrow stripe slanting to the right, using 2 colours coded as A and B.
Using A, make 29ch.
1st row Into 3rd ch from hook work 1dc, 1dc into each ch to end. Turn. 28dc.
Commence striped patt.
1st row (RS) Using A, 1ch to count as first dc, miss first dc, 1dc into next dc joining in B on last loop, *using B, work 1dc into each of next 2dc joining in A on last loop, using A, work 1dc into each of next 2dc joining in B on last loop, rep from * to last 2 sts, using B, work 1dc into each of last 2dc. Turn.
2nd row Using B, 1ch to count as first dc, miss first dc, 1dc into next dc joining in A on last loop, *using A, work 1dc into each of next 2dc joining in B on last loop, using B, work 1dc into each of next 2dc joining in A on last loop, rep from * to last 2 sts, using A, work 1dc into each of last 2dc. Turn.
3rd row Using A, 1ch to count as first dc, miss first dc, *using B, work 1dc into each of next 2dc joining in A on last loop, using A, work

1dc into each of next 2dc joining in B on last loop, rep from * to last 3 sts, using B, work 1dc into each of next 2dc joining in A on last loop, using A, work 1dc into last dc. Turn.
4th row Using A, 1ch to count as first dc, miss first dc, *using B, work 1dc into each of next 2dc joining in A on last loop, using A, work 1dc into each of next 2dc joining in B on last loop, rep from * to last 3 sts, using B, work 1dc into each of next 2dc joining in A on last loop, using A, work 1dc into last dc. Turn.
5th row Using B, 1ch to count as first dc, miss first dc, 1dc into next dc joining in A on last loop, *using A, work 1dc into each of next 2dc joining in B on last loop, using B, work 1dc into each of next 2dc joining in A on last loop, rep from * to last 2 sts, using A, work 1dc into each of last 2dc. Turn.
6th row Using A, 1ch to count as first dc, miss first dc, 1dc into next dc joining in B on last loop, *using B, work 1dc into each of next 2dc joining in A on last loop, using A, work 1dc into each of next 2dc joining in B on last loop, rep from * to last 2 sts, using B, work 1dc into each of last 2dc. Turn.
7th row Using B, 1ch to count as first dc, miss first dc, *using A, work 1dc into each of next 2dc joining in B on last loop, using B, work 1dc into each of next 2dc joining in A on last loop, rep from * to last 3 sts, using A, work 1dc into each of next 2dc joining in B on last loop, using B, work 1dc into last dc. Turn.
8th row Using B, 1ch to count as first dc, miss first dc, *using A, work 1dc into each of next 2dc joining in B on last loop, using B, work 1dc into each of next 2dc joining in A on last loop, rep from * to last 3 sts, using A, work 1dc into each of next 2dc joining in B on last loop, using B, work 1dc into last dc. Turn.
These 8 rows form the pattern.

Chevron stripes

These are worked in the same way as horizontal stripes, using an even number of rows and as many colours as required. If more than 3 colours are used, however, it is advisable to break off the yarn at the end of each stripe, rather than carry it up the side of the work until it is required again. This sample is worked in 3 colours, coded as A, B and C.
Using A, make 38ch.
1st row (RS) Into 3rd ch from hook work 1dc, 1dc into each of next 6ch, 3dc into next ch, 1dc into each of next 8ch, insert hook into next ch and draw loop through, miss 1ch, insert hook into next ch and draw loop through, yrh and draw through 3 all loops on hook, 1dc into each of next 8ch, 3dc into next ch, 1dc into each of last 8ch. Turn.
2nd row 1ch to count as first dc, (insert hook into next dc and draw loop through) into each of next 2dc, yrh and draw through all 3 loops on hook, 1dc into each of next 6dc, 3dc into next dc, 1dc into each of next 8dc, insert hook into next dc and draw loop through, miss 1dc, insert hook into next dc and draw loop through, yrh and draw through all 3 loops on hook, 1dc into each of next 8dc, 3dc into next dc, 1dc into each of next 6dc, (insert hook into next dc and draw loop through) into each of next 2dc, yrh and draw through all 3 loops on hook, 1dc into last dc. Turn.
The 2nd row forms the pattern. Work in stripes of 2 rows B, 2 rows C and 2 rows A throughout.

Horizontal stripe

Check pattern

Yarn across back

Using separate balls

Diagonal stripes

Chevron stripes

Jacquard & patchwork

Small jacquard designs, such as squares and diamonds, may be used to produce an all-over pattern or a large, single motif can be used most effectively to highlight a plain background. Random patchwork effects can also be used to produce a most interesting and original fabric.

An all-over jacquard pattern may be worked by carrying the yarn not in use across the back of the fabric but for single motifs and patchwork patterns, separate balls of yarn should be used for each colour. In both methods, each new colour must be bought into use correctly, as

shown in the previous Chapter.
Basic stitches, such as double crochet, half trebles or trebles should be used for these patterns, otherwise the definition of the motif, or patches, will be lost.

Jacquard patterns
Just as in knitting, these motifs may be worked from a chart where each colour in the pattern is shown as a separate symbol, or from row-by-row instructions where each colour is coded with

a letter, such as A and B. The method used is largely a matter of personal choice. The first sample shown here gives row instructions only and in the 2 following samples, the first few rows are given out in full and the motif is then

completed from the appropriate chart—in this way you will soon become familiar with both methods.

Square jacquard pattern
This pattern requires multiples of 7 plus 3 and 2 extra turning chain, using 2 colours coded as A and B. Using A, make 26ch.
1st row (RS) Into 4th ch from hook work 1tr, 1tr into each ch to end. Turn. 24tr.

2nd row 3ch to count as first tr, miss first tr, 1tr into each tr to end. Turn.
3rd row Using A, 3ch to count as first tr, miss first tr, work 1tr into each of next 2tr joining in B on last loop, *using B, work 1tr into each of next 4tr joining in A on last loop, using A, work

1tr into each of next 3tr joining in B on last loop, rep from * to end but do not join in B at end of last rep. Turn.
4th row As 3rd.
These 4 rows form the pattern.

Diamond jacquard pattern
This pattern requires multiples of 6 plus 1 and 2 extra turning chain, using 2 colours coded as A and B. Using A, make 33ch.
1st row (RS) Using A, into 4th ch from hook work 1tr, 1tr into next ch joining in B on last loop, *using B, work 1tr into next ch joining in A on last loop, using A, work 1tr into each of

next 5ch joining in B on last loop, rep from * to last 4ch, using B, work 1tr into next ch joining in A on last loop, using A, work 1tr into each of last 3ch. Turn. 31tr.
2nd row Using A, 3ch to count as first tr, miss first tr, 1tr into next tr joining in B on last loop, *using B, work 1tr into each of next 3tr joining in A on last loop, using A, work 1tr into each

of next 3tr joining in B on last loop, rep from * to last 5 sts, using B, work 1tr into each of next 3tr joining in A on last loop, using A, work 1tr into next tr, 1tr into 3rd of first 3ch. Turn.
Continue in pattern as given in chart below, repeating 10 rows for required length.

Butterfly motif
Work out the position for the motif against a double crochet background, allowing 26 sts and 28 rows to complete the butterfly.
1st row (RS) Using A, 1ch to count as first dc, miss first dc, 1dc into each of next 13dc joining

in B on last loop, using B, work 1dc into each of next 3dc joining in A on last loop, using A, work 1dc into each of next 9dc. Turn.
2nd row Using A, 1ch to count as first dc, miss first dc, 1dc into each of next 7dc joining in B on last loop, using B, work 1dc into each of

next 6dc joining in A on last loop, using A, work 1dc into each of next 4dc joining in C on last loop, using C, work 1dc into each of next 2dc joining in A on last loop, using A, work 1dc into each of next 6dc. Turn.
Continue working in pattern as given in chart.

Patchwork patterns
Although patchwork fabrics may appear complicated, they are quite simple to work. Each patch is worked over the same number of stitches and rows but the order in which the different patches and colours are used gives each section a completely different appearance.
The patches can be worked in a continuous strip to the required length and the required number of strips may then be joined together to form pram and cot covers, cushion covers or afghans and blankets. A really colourful effect can be achieved by using oddments of yarn. The sample shown here has been worked in 6 colours, coded as A, B, C, D, E and F, using a Double Knitting yarn and a No.4.00 (ISR) crochet hook, to give each patch a width of 10cm (*4in*) and a depth of 10cm (*4in*).
1st patch
Using A, make 18ch.
1st row (RS) Into 4th ch from hook work 1tr, 1tr into each ch to end. Turn. 16tr.
2nd row 3ch to count as first tr, miss first tr, 1tr into each tr to end. Turn.
Rep 2nd row 6 times more. Fasten off.
2nd patch
1st row Join in B and work 2nd row as given for 1st patch.
2nd row Using B, as 1st row.
Rep these 2 rows 3 times more, using C, D and E. Fasten off.
3rd patch
1st row Join in F, 3ch to count as first tr, miss

first tr, work 1tr into each of next 17tr joining in A on last loop, using A, work 1tr into each of next 8tr. Turn.
2nd row Using A, 3ch to count as first tr, miss first tr, work 1tr into each of next 7tr joining in F on last loop, using F, work 1tr into each of next 8tr. Turn.
Rep last 2 rows once more. Break off F and A.
5th row Join in B, 3ch to count as first tr, miss first tr, work 1tr into each of next 7tr joining in C on last loop, using C, work 1tr into each of next 8tr. Turn.
6th row Using C, 3ch to count as first tr, miss first tr, work 1tr into each of next 7tr joining in B on last loop, using B, work 1tr into each of next 8tr. Turn.
Rep last 2 rows once more. Fasten off.
4th patch
1st row Join in D and work 2nd row as given for 1st patch. Turn.
Rep last row 3 times more. Break off D.
5th row Join in E and F and work 1st row as given for 3rd patch.
6th row Using F and E work 2nd row as given for 3rd patch.
Rep last 2 rows once more. Fasten off.
These 4 patches form the pattern and are repeated throughout for the required length, varying the order in which they are worked and the colours used on each subsequent patch. Make as many more strips as are needed in the same way, again varying the sequence in which the patches are worked and the colours used for each patch.

COLOUR KEY □ A ⊠ B

REP 6 STS

Butterfly motif

COLOUR KEY

☐	A
☒	B
⊡	C
◫	D
◩	E
⊡	F

27 25 23 21 19 17 15 13 11 9 7 5 3 1

PATT OVER 26 STS

Square jacquard pattern

Diamond jacquard pattern

Patchwork

Filet crochet

The word 'filet' means 'net' and this form of crochet is one of the simplest to work to produce a lacy fabric with numerous uses. It is made up of two basic stitches—the chain and the treble. The trebles are worked in groups to produce a solid block and the spaces between each block are formed by chains, to correspond with the number of trebles over which each space is worked.

Many beautiful and intricate designs can be incorporated into this method, working from a chart as given for the motifs in Chapter 26, or a simple all-over net fabric may be produced.

Basic filet net

This is formed by a single treble with a 2 chain space between each treble. Make a chain having multiples of 3 plus one and an extra 4 chain, e.g., 32ch.

1st row (RS) Into 8th ch from hook work 1tr, noting that the 7 missed ch form a 2ch space on the lower edge, 3ch to count as the first tr and another 2ch space along the top edge, *2ch, miss 3ch, 1tr into next ch, rep from * to end. Turn.

2nd row 5ch to count as first tr and 2ch space, miss first tr and 2ch space, 1tr into next tr, * 2ch, miss 2ch space, 1tr into next tr, rep from * working last tr into 5th of first 7ch. Turn. The 2nd row forms the pattern, ending each subsequent row with 1tr into 3rd of first 5ch.

Blocks and spaces

On to this basic net background, simple or more complicated patterns of blocks and spaces may now be built up.

Blocks worked over spaces.

These are formed by working 1tr into the corresponding tr of the previous row, 2tr into the next 2ch space and 1tr in to the next tr, forming a block of 4tr, the last of which belongs to the next space.

Spaces worked over blocks.

These are formed by working 1tr into the first tr of the block, 2ch, miss the next 2tr and work 1tr into the last tr of the block.

To begin a first row with a block.

Make 3 extra ch to count as the first tr and work the next tr into the 4th ch from hook, then complete the first block of 4tr by working 1tr into each of the next 2ch.

To begin a first row with a space.

Make 7 extra ch to count as the 2ch space along the lower edge, the first tr and 2ch space along top edge, then work the next tr into the 8th ch from hook.

tr, rep from * working last tr into 5th of first 7ch. Turn.

3rd row 5ch to count as first tr and 2ch space, miss first 3tr, *1tr into next tr, 2ch, miss 2ch space, 1tr into next tr, 2ch, miss 2tr, rep from * to end, 1tr into 3rd of first 3ch. Turn.

4th row 5ch to count as given for 3rd row, *1tr into next tr, 2tr into 2ch space, 1tr into next tr, 2ch, miss 2ch space, rep from * to end, 1tr into 3rd of first 5ch. Turn.

5th row 5ch to count as 3rd row, miss 2ch space, *1tr into next tr, 2ch, miss 2tr, 1tr into next tr, 2ch, miss 2ch space, rep from * to end,

working last tr into 3rd of first 5ch.
The 2nd to 5th rows form the pattern.

Filet pattern using double blocks

Make a chain having multiples of 12 plus 7 and 2 extra chain, e.g., 33ch.

1st row Into 4th ch from hook work 1tr, 1tr into each of next 5ch, *2ch, miss 2ch, 1tr into next ch, 2ch, miss 2ch, 1tr into each of next 7ch, rep from * to end. Turn.

2nd row 3ch to count as first tr, miss first tr, 1tr into each of next 6tr, *2ch, miss 2ch, 1tr into next tr, 2ch, miss 2ch, 1tr into each of next

Simple pattern of alternating blocks and spaces

Make a chain having multiples of 6 plus 4 and an extra 4 chain, e.g. 32ch.

1st row (RS) As 1st row of basic filet net.

2nd row 3ch to count as first tr, 2tr into 2ch space, 1tr into next tr, *2ch, miss 2ch space, 1tr into next tr, 2tr into 2ch space, 1tr into next

7tr, rep from * to end working last tr into 3rd of first 3ch. Turn.

3rd row 5ch to count as first tr and 2ch, miss first 3tr, 1tr into next tr, 2ch, miss 2tr, 1tr into next tr, **(2tr into next 2ch space, 1tr into next tr) twice, (2ch, miss 2tr, 1tr into next tr)

twice, rep from * to end, working last tr into 3rd of first 3ch. Turn.

4th row 5ch to count as first tr and 2ch, miss first tr and 2ch, 1tr into next tr, 2ch, miss 2ch, *1tr into each of next 7tr, 2ch, miss 2ch, 1tr into next tr, 2ch, miss 2ch, rep from * to end, 1tr into 3rd of first 5ch. Turn.

5th row 3ch to count as first tr, miss first tr, 2tr into first space, 1tr into next tr, 2tr into next space, 1tr into next tr *(2ch, miss 2tr, 1tr into next tr) twice, (2tr into next space, 1tr into next tr) twice, rep from * to end, working last tr into 3rd of first 5ch. Turn.

The 2nd to 5th rows form the pattern.

Shaping in filet crochet

Attractive borders for household linens may be worked which have an interesting serrated edge. This is achieved by decreasing or increasing blocks or spaces at a given point.

To increase a block at the beginning of a row

Make 5ch, into the 4th ch from hook work 1tr, 1tr into next ch then work 1tr into the last st of the previous row. One block has been increased.

To increase two blocks

Make 8ch, into 4th ch from hook work 1tr, 1tr into each of next 4ch then work 1tr into the last st of the previous row.

To increase a space at the beginning of a row

Make 7ch to count as (2ch space at the end of the previous row, 3 to count as the first tr of the new row and another 2 for the top of the space between the first tr and the next st of the previous row), 1tr into first tr of the row (edge st).

To increase a block at the end of a row

Make provision for the increase at the beginning of the previous row by working 7ch, miss first ch and ss into each of next 3ch, noting that the remaining 3ch will count as the first tr of the row being worked, then continue in pattern to the end of the row. At the end of the following row, where the increase is required, work 1tr into each of the 3ss. One block has been increased.

To increase a space at the end of a row

Work as given for increasing a block at the end of a row but when the position for the increase is reached, miss next 2ss, 2ch, work 1tr into last ss. One space has been increased.

To decrease a block or a space at the beginning of a row

Ss across each of the first 3 sts and into the 4th st, make 3ch to count as the first tr or 5ch to count as the first tr and 2ch space, then continue in pattern. One block or space has been decreased.

To decrease a block or space at the end of a row

Work in pattern to within the last block or space, then turn and miss these stitches and continue in pattern for the next row.

Simple filet edging

This edging is worked by using the exact number of stitches to give the width and continuing until it is the required length. Make 17ch.

1st row (RS) Into 8th ch from hook work 1tr, 1tr into each of next 3ch, (2ch, miss 2ch, 1tr into next ch) twice. Turn.

2nd row 5ch to count as first tr and 2ch space, miss first tr and 2ch space, 1tr into next tr, 2tr into 2ch space, 1tr into next tr, 2ch, miss next 2tr, 1tr into next tr, turn, noting that one space has been decreased.

3rd row 7ch to increase one space, 1tr into first tr, 2tr into 2ch space, 1tr into next tr, 2ch, miss next 2tr, 1tr into next tr, 2ch, 1tr into 3rd of first 5ch. Turn.

The 2nd and 3rd rows form the pattern.

Looped & woven fabrics

Fun-fur fabrics can be produced either by means of loop stitches, chain stitches or by applying cut ends of yarn to a mesh background. Any of these methods can be used for an all-over fabric or separate bands can be worked as collars and cuffs. They are fun to work and they all provide a thick, warm fabric, particularly suitable for pram or cot covers. Worked in a thick, soft cotton they also make ideal bath or nursery rugs.

A simple filet background may be used to achieve interesting woven fabrics, either by threading yarn in contrast colours through each chain space of the background, or by applying vertical chains directly on to the background.

Loop fur stitch

Each loop is formed round the 1st and 2nd fingers of the left hand on the back of the fabric as it is worked. The position of each loop can be placed one above the other into every stitch on every alternate row, to give a dense fabric, or they can be worked into every alternate stitch and into the stitches between the loops on the following alternate row, to form a thinner fabric.

To work this sample make 31ch.

1st row (RS) Into 3rd ch from hook work 1dc, 1dc into each ch to end. Turn. 30dc.

2nd row 1ch to count as first dc, miss first dc, *insert hook into next dc, hold yarn across 1st and 2nd fingers of left hand and extend yarn to required height by lifting 2nd finger, keeping hook to the right of the yarn over the finger place hook over yarn lying between 2nd and 3rd fingers and draw loop through dc, keeping hook to the left of the loop over the finger yrh from main ball of yarn and draw through both loops on hook, remove 2nd finger from loop—called loop 1—, rep from * to last dc, 1dc into last dc. Turn.

3rd row 1ch to count as first dc, miss first dc, 1dc into each st to end. Turn.

The 2nd and 3rd rows form the pattern.

Chain fur stitch

Here the fur effect is formed by chains which are worked across the back of the fabric, to give a close, curly texture.

To work this sample make 32ch.

1st row (RS) Into 4th ch from hook work 1tr, 1tr into each ch to end. Turn. 30tr.

2nd row 1ch to count as first dc, miss first tr, *1dc into back loop only of next tr, 10ch, rep from * to end working last dc into 3rd of first 3ch. Turn.

3rd row 3ch to count as first tr, miss first dc, *1tr into the missed loop of the next tr of the previous alternate row, rep from * to end working last tr into first ch of last row. Turn.

The 2nd and 3rd rows form the pattern.

Cut fur stitch

This method requires a mesh background, into which separate, cut ends of yarn are looped. As with loop fur stitch, the thickness of the fabric may be altered by the positioning of the loops and the number of strands of yarn which are used. To work this sample make 32ch for the mesh background.

1st row (RS) Into 4th ch from hook work 1dc, *1ch, miss 1ch, 1dc into next ch, rep from * to end. Turn.

2nd row 1ch to count as first dc, 1ch, *1dc into next 1ch space, 1ch, rep from * to end, 1dc into 2nd of first 3ch. Turn.

The 2nd row forms the pattern, noting that on subsequent rows the last dc is worked into first ch.

To add the loops. First cut yarn into 12.5cm (5in) lengths. Take 2 strands of yarn and fold in half. With RS of mesh background facing, insert hook horizontally under the first dc of the 1st row, put the folded loop of yarn over the hook and draw through the work, place the 4 ends of yarn over the hook and draw through loops on hook, then pull up tightly to secure. Repeat into every dc, or every alternate dc, as required.

Woven fabrics

The methods shown here can be used to produce colourful plaid effects, which are ideal for travelling rugs and afghans. Oddments of the same thickness of yarn may be used for the applied vertical stripes and the background fabric shown here is a simple filet net. Instructions for this can be found in the previous section, on page 22.

Using woven strands of yarn

Make a simple filet net background to the required width and length, as given in Chapter 11 but having a single treble with 1 chain space between each treble instead of 2 chain spaces. Cut lengths of yarn to the same length as the background, allowing approximately 15.0cm (6in) extra at each end for fringing. Take 2 or 3 strands together at a time and with RS of background facing, begin at lower right hand corner. Thread yarn under first chain in 1st row, over first chain in 2nd row, then continue in this way to top right hand corner. Begin again at lower edge, take yarn over 2nd chain in 1st row, under 2nd chain in 2nd row, then continue in this way to top edge. Repeat into each space across fabric, varying colours as required.

Using crochet chains of yarn

Make a simple filet net background as given when using woven strands of yarn, to the required width and length. Using 2 balls of yarn together in colours as required, make a slip loop and place on hook. With RS of filet background facing, begin at lower right hand corner and hold yarn at back of work, insert hook into first chain space in 1st row to back of work, yarn round hook then draw loop through to front of work and through loop on hook. Continue in this way, working into each chain space to top edge. Fasten off securely. Begin again at lower edge and work in same way into each of the 2nd chain spaces to the top edge. Repeat into each chain space across fabric.

Woven plaid fabric

This requires a filet background to the required width and length, using groups of two blocks of 2 trebles and two 1 chain spaces worked above each other throughout. Make a number of chain divisible by 8 plus 5 and 2 extra turning chain, e.g., 31ch.

1st row Into 4th ch from hook work 1tr, 1tr into each of next 3ch, *(1ch, miss 1ch, 1tr into next ch) twice, 1tr into each of next 4ch, rep from * to end. Turn.

2nd row 3ch to count as first tr, miss first tr, 1tr into each of next 4tr, *(1ch, miss 1ch space, 1tr into next tr) twice, 1tr into each of next 4tr, rep from * to end working last tr into 3rd of first 3ch. Turn.

Rep the 2nd row for the required length, working in stripes of 4 rows of one colour and 2 rows of contrast colour throughout.

Using two or three strands of yarn together, beg in at lower right hand corner and weave yarn over and under each chain as given for first woven sample, using first colour for first pair of chain spaces and second colour for second pair throughout.

This fabric can be adapted in many different ways by varying the number of blocks and chain spaces and also the number of colours used.

Loop fur stitch

Chain fur stitch

Cut fur stitch

Woven fabric using strands of yarn

Woven fabric using crochet chains of yarn

Woven plaid fabric

Irish crochet

Irish crochet

There are two distinct types of Irish crochet, which both have different working methods. The traditional form is the heavier of the two and each motif, or 'sprig', is worked separately over a length of yarn to give it an almost three dimensional effect and then joined together into an all-over pattern by means of a net background, called 'filling'.

The finer version, sometimes called 'baby Irish crochet' because it was so often used to trim elaborate layettes, is worked continuously into square or circular sections, beginning with a central motif around which a filling is then worked. Each section is then joined together with a series of picot bars or smaller motifs.

Traditional Irish crochet

To work the authentic method, it is first necessary to plan the shape and size of fabric required by tracing out the design on a piece of strong paper or linen. As each separate motif is completed, it should be tacked into position on the plan. The motifs are then joined together by a filling of chains, or picot bars, to form an all-over fabric. A much simpler method, however, is to work the background first to the required size and then apply the separate motifs directly on to the net.

Here we give samples of 2 net fillings and a selection of sprigs.

Honeycomb filling

This simple net background requires multiples of 4 chain plus 1 and 5 extra turning chain. When working to a plan, as each sprig is reached, join it by means of a slip stitch where it touches the filling.

1st row Into 10th ch from hook work 1dc, *6ch, miss 3ch, 1dc into next ch, rep from * to end. Turn.

2nd row 9ch, 1dc into first 6ch space of previous row, *6ch, 1dc into next 6ch space, rep from * to end working last dc into 9ch loop. Turn.

The 2nd row forms the pattern.

Diamond picot filling

This net background is joined as given for honeycomb filling and requires multiples of 4 chain plus 1 and 6 extra turning chain.

1st row Into 3rd ch from hook work 1dc to form picot, 1ch, miss 7ch, 1dc into next ch, *(4ch, 1dc into 3rd ch from hook to form picot) twice, 1ch, miss 3ch of foundation row, 1dc into next ch, rep from * to end. Turn.

2nd row 7ch, 1dc into 3rd ch from hook, 1ch, 1dc into 1ch space between picots in next loop, *(4ch, 1dc into 3rd ch from hook to form picot) twice, 1ch, 1dc into 1ch space between picots of next loop, rep from * to end working last dc into last ch space after picot on end loop. Turn.

The 2nd row forms the pattern.

Irish crochet rings

First estimate the length of separate thread required to complete a ring. Coil the separate thread into a ring by winding it 2 or 3 times round a finger. Working from front to back through the ring, join in the correct yarn with a slip stitch, then work 1 round of double crochet into the ring. Join with a slip stitch to first double crochet to complete the ring.

Where a series of rings are required, complete half of the first ring only, continue working in double crochet over the separate thread until the next position is reached, then coil the yarn and complete half of the 2nd ring only. Continue in this way until the required number of rings have been formed, then complete each ring by working the 2nd half, slip stitching along the length of thread between each ring.

Irish crochet rose motif

Using the correct yarn, coil the end 3 or 4 times round a finger, remove the ring and secure with a slip stitch.

1st round 2ch to count as first dc, work 17dc into ring. Join with a ss to 2nd of first 2ch. 18dc.

2nd round 6ch, miss 2dc, 1htr into next dc, *4ch, miss 2dc, 1htr into next dc, rep from * 3 times more, 4ch, miss last 2dc, Join with a ss to 2nd of first 6ch. 6 loops.

3rd round Into each 4ch space work (1dc, 1htr, 3tr, 1htr, 1dc). Join with a ss to first dc. 6 petals.

4th round Ss into back of nearest htr of 2nd round, *5ch, pass ch behind petal of previous round and ss into back of next htr of 2nd round rep from * 5 times more working last ss into same htr as first ss.

5th round Into each 5ch space work (1dc, 1htr, 5tr, 1htr, 1dc). Join with a ss to first dc.

6th round Ss into back of ss of 4th round, *6ch, pass ch behind petal of previous round and ss into back of next ss of 4th round, rep from * 5 times more working last ss into same place as first ss.

7th round Into each 6ch space work (1dc, 1htr, 7tr, 1htr, 1dc). Join with a ss to first dc. Fasten off.

Irish crochet shamrock motif

Estimate the length of separate yarn required, allowing enough to form the stem. Using correct yarn make 16ch.

1st round Into 16th ch from hook work 1dc, (15ch, 1dc into same ch as last dc) twice.

2nd round Working over separate length of yarn work 22dc into each 15ch loop. Join with a ss to first dc. 3 petals.

3rd round Working over separate length of yarn, *miss first dc of petal, 1dc into each of next 20dc, miss last dc of petal, rep from * twice more. Join with a ss to first dc.

4th round Make 25ch to form stem, working over separate length of yarn into 2nd ch from hook work 1dc, 1dc into each ch to end. Join with a ss to first dc on first petal. Fasten off.

Fine Irish crochet

The samples shown here give 2 methods of joining. The first incorporates a net background to form a square motif. The second forms a round motif and these are then joined together with a smaller motif. Both examples may be used to produce exquisite place mats, tray cloths or tablecloths.

Shamrock and crown medallion

Make 16ch.

1st round Into 16ch from hook work 1dc, (15ch, 1dc into same ch as first dc) twice.

2nd round Work 24dc into each ch loop. Join with a ss to first dc.

3rd round Work 1dc into each dc. Join with a ss to first dc.

4th round Ss into each of next 3dc counting join as 4th ss, **1dc into next dc, *4ch, 1dc into 3rd ch from hook to form picot, 5ch, 1dc into 3rd ch from hook to form picot, 1ch— called 1 picot loop—, miss 4dc, 1dc into next dc, rep from * twice more. 1 picot loop, miss 4dc of first leaf and 4dc of next leaf of shamrock, rep from ** ending with 1 picot loop. Join with a ss to first dc. 12 picot loops.

5th round Ss into centre of first picot loop between picots, 1dc into same loop, *8ch, 1dc between picots of next picot loop, turn, 1ss into loop just made, 3ch, 9tr into same loop, 4ch, turn, miss first 2tr, 1tr into next tr, **1ch, miss 1tr, 1tr into next tr, rep from ** twice more, 1ch, miss 1tr, 1tr into top of 3ch, 4ch, 1dc into 3rd ch from hook, 2ch, 1dc into same loop, (4ch, 1dc into 3rd ch from hook, 5ch, 1dc into 3rd ch from hook, 2ch, 1dc between picots of next picot loop) twice, rep from * omitting 1dc at end of last rep. Join with a ss to first dc.

6th round Ss up side of tr and into each of next 3ch, 1dc into same space, *4ch, 1dc into 3rd ch from hook, 5ch, 1dc into 3rd ch from hook, 2ch, miss 1 space, 1dc into next space, 4ch, 1dc into 3rd ch from hook, 5ch, 1dc into 3rd ch from hook, 2ch, miss 2 spaces, 1dc into next space, (4ch, 1dc into 3rd ch from hook, 5ch, 1dc into 3rd ch from hook, 2ch, 1dc between picots of next loop) twice, 4ch, 1dc into 3rd ch from hook, 5ch, 1dc into 3rd ch from hook, 2ch, 1dc into first space of next block, rep from * omitting 1dc at end of last rep. Join with a ss to first dc.

7th round Ss into centre of first picot loop, 1dc into same loop, *8ch, 1dc between picots of next loop, turn, 1ss into loop just made, 3ch, 9tr into same loop, 1tr into next dc, 4ch, turn, miss 2tr, 1tr into next tr, **1ch, miss 1tr, 1tr into next tr, rep from ** twice more, 1ch, miss 1tr, 1tr into top of 3ch, 4ch, 1dc into 3rd ch from hook, 2ch, 1dc into same loop, (4ch, 1dc into 3rd ch from hook, 5ch, 1dc into 3rd ch from hook, 2ch, 1dc between picots of next loop) 4 times, rep from * omitting 1dc at end of last rep. Join with a ss to first dc.

8th round Ss up side of tr and into each of next 3ch, 1dc into first space, *4ch, 1dc into 3rd ch from hook, 5ch, 1dc into 3rd ch from hook, 2ch, miss 1 space, 1dc into next space, 4ch, 1dc into 3rd ch from hook, 5ch, 1dc into 3rd ch from hook, 2ch, miss 2 spaces, 1dc into next loop, (4ch, 1dc into 3rd ch from hook, 5ch, 1dc into 3rd ch from hook, 2ch, 1dc between picots of next loop) 4 times, 4ch, 1dc into 3rd ch from hook, 5ch, 1dc into 3rd ch from hook, 2ch, 1dc into first space of next block, rep from * omitting 1dc at end of last rep. Join with a ss to first dc. Fasten off.

Wheel motif

Make 8ch. Join with a ss to first ch to form circle.

1st round Work 18dc into circle. Do not join.

2nd round *1dc into each of next 2dc, 2dc into next dc, rep from * 5 times more. Do not join. 24 dc.

3rd round *1dc into each of next 3dc, 2dc into next dc, rep from * 5 times more. 30dc. Cont inc in this way on next 3 rounds. Join with a ss to first dc. 48dc.

7th round 1dc into same place as ss, *5ch, miss 1dc, 1dc into next dc, rep from * ending with 2ch, 1tr into first dc. 24 loops.

8th and 9th rounds *5ch, 1dc into next loop, rep from * ending with 2ch, 1tr into tr of previous round.

10th round *10ch, miss 1 loop, 1dc into next loop, rep from * to end, 10ch. Join with a ss to tr of previous round.

11th round Work 15dc into each 10ch loop. Join with a ss to first dc.

12th round 1dc into same place as ss, 1dc into each of next 6dc, *into next dc work (1dc, 3ch, 1dc, 5ch, 1dc, 3ch, 1dc), 1dc into each of next 14dc, rep from * ending last rep with 1dc into each of last 7dc. Join with a ss to first dc. Fasten off.

Work 2nd motif in same way for first 11 rounds.

12th round (joining round) 1dc into same place as ss, 1dc into each of next 6dc, *into next ds work 1dc, 3ch, 1dc, 2ch, ss into corresponding 5ch loop on 1st motif, 2ch, 1dc, 3ch and 1dc into same dc of 2nd motif, *, 1dc into each of next 14dc, rep from * to *, then complete as given for 1st motif.

Joining motifs

Make 6ch. Join with a ss to first ch to form circle.

1st round Work 8dc into circle. Join with a ss to first dc.

2nd round 1dc into same place as ss, *4ch, 1dc into next dc, rep from * ending with 1ch, 1tr into first dc. 8 loops.

3rd round *5ch, 1dc into next loop, 10ch, 1dc into next loop, rep from * ending with ss into tr of previous round.

4th round *5dc into next 5ch loop, 6dc into next 10ch loop, ss into 5th ch on free picot between motifs, 6dc into same 10ch loop, rep from * to end. Join with a ss to first dc. Fasten off.

Top to bottom: Wheel motif; Diamond picot filling; Irish crochet rings; Rose motif; Shamrock motif; Shamrock and crown medallion; Honeycomb filling

Tunisian crochet

This interesting technique is a combination of both knitting and crochet, worked on a single, long hook instead of a pair of needles. Although the overall term applies to this method of working, it is very often referred to as 'Afghan stitch'. This is rather misleading, as it implies that only one stitch is used, instead of the numerous and varied stitches which form most attractive fabrics.

This technique begins in the same way as crochet, with the required length of chains and a working loop on the hook. When making the

initial length of chains, you will not require any extra chains for turning—a chain length of 20 will give you exactly 20 working stitches. The first row is worked from right to left into each chain, keeping the last loop of each stitch on the hook, then the 2nd row, which is, in fact, the completion of the 1st row, is worked back again from left to right without turning the work, reducing the loops along the row until only the working loop remains. With this method, the right side of the work is always facing you. The fabric produced is very strong and hard-

wearing and, depending on the stitch used, the finished appearance can resemble crochet or look deceptively like knitting. Because of the working method, Tunisian crochet sometimes produces as bias effect but this tendency can be overcome by working the stitches fairly loosely. Always pull the yarn round the hook adequately through the stitch and, when working back along a row from left to right, never pull the first stitch through so tightly that you flatten the height of the row.

Plain or basic Tunisian stitch
Make any number of chain.
1st row Insert hook into 2nd ch from hook, yrh and draw loop through ch, *insert hook into next ch, yrh and draw loop through ch, rep from * to end. Do not turn work. The number of loops on the hook should be the same

as the commencing ch.
2nd row Working from left to right, yrh and draw through first loop on hook, *yrh and draw through 2 loops on hook, rep from * to end. Do not turn work. Working loop only remains on hook.
3rd row *Insert hook from right to left behind

the vertical thread of the next st, yrh and draw loop through, rep from * into each vertical thread to end. Do not turn.
4th row As 2nd.
The 3rd and 4th rows form the pattern, always ending with a 4th row.

Tunisian treble stitch
Make any number of chain.
1st row Yrh, insert hook into 3rd ch from hook, yrh and draw loop through ch, yrh and draw through 2 loops on hook, *yrh, insert hook into next ch, yrh and draw loop through ch, yrh

and draw through 2 loops on hook, rep from * to end. Do not turn.
2nd row As 2nd row of basic Tunisian stitch.
3rd row 1ch to count as first st, *yrh, insert hook from right to left behind vertical thread of the next st, yrh and draw loop through, yrh

and draw through 2 loops on hook, rep from * to end. Do not turn.
4th row As 2nd.
The 3rd and 4th rows form the pattern, always ending with a 4th row.

Tunisian stocking stitch
Make any number of chain. Work 1st and 2nd rows as given for basic Tunisian stitch.
3rd row *Insert hook from front to back

between vertical threads and below top edge of next st of previous row, yrh and draw loop through fairly loosely, rep from * to end. Do not turn.

4th row As 2nd.
The 3rd and 4th rows form the pattern, always ending with a 4th row.

Tunisian cluster stitch
Make a number of chain divisible by 8 plus 5. Work 1st, 2nd and 3rd rows as given for basic Tunisian stitch.
4th row Yrh and draw through 3 loops, *3ch, yrh and draw through 5 loops, (i.e. the loop on

the hook and the next 4 loops), rep from * to last 2 loops, 3ch, yrh and draw through rem 3 loops, (i.e. the loop on the hook and rem 2 loops). Do not turn.
5th row *Insert hook into each of next 3ch and draw a loop through each, insert hook into top

of cluster and draw a loop through, rep from * to end drawing the last loop through the edge st. Do not turn.
6th row As 2nd.
The 3rd to 6th rows form the pattern, always ending with a 4th or 6th row.

Shaping in Tunisian crochet
These fabrics can be shaped to make garments, just as with knitting and crochet. The usual methods are given here, together with instructions for making buttonholes.
Increasing a stitch at the right hand edge
To increase one stitch at the right hand edge, make one chain then insert the hook behind the vertical thread of the first stitch, (edge stitch), yrh and draw loop through, continue in pattern to the end of the row.
Increasing a stitch at the left hand edge
To increase one stitch at the left hand edge, this must be worked on a even numbered row. Yrh and draw through one loop, 1ch, *yrh and draw through 2 loops, rep from * to the end of the row. On the next row patt to the last stitch,

insert hook into the 1ch and draw a loop through, insert hook into the last stitch and draw a loop through.
Increasing 2 or more stitches at the right hand edge
Make the required number of chain then work basic stitch into each chain and the first vertical thread (edge stitch) and continue in pattern to end.
Increasing 2 or more stitches at the left hand edge
Using a separate length of yarn make the required number of chain and leave for time being. Work in pattern to the end of the row then work in basic stitch into each of the separate chain.

Decreasing one stitch at the right hand edge
Insert the hook behind 2 vertical threads, yrh and draw through one loop only, continue in pattern to the end of the row.
Decreasing one stitch at the left hand edge
Work as given for decreasing at the right hand edge by inserting the hook behind the last 2 vertical threads together, yrh and draw through one loop only.
Working a buttonhole
Work in pattern from right to left to the position where the buttonhole is required, wind the yarn round the hook for the required number of stitches for the buttonhole, miss this number of stitches in the previous row and continue in pattern to end. On the following row, work off each loop of yarn as if it were a stitch.

Basic Tunisian stitch

Increasing 2 or more stitches at right hand edge

Tunisian treble stitch

Increasing 2 or more sts at left hand edge

Tunisian stocking stitch

Tunisian cluster stitch

Decreasing 1 stitch at right hand edge

Increasing 1 stitch at right hand edge

First step of working a buttonhole

Increasing 1 stitch at left hand edge

Working a buttonhole

Aran crochet

Crochet stitches can be combined to form fabrics which have the appearance of Aran patterns. The patterns can be built up against a plain background, either in the row-by-row working instructions or by applying surface stitches to the background when it has been completed.

The fabric formed has a raised, three-dimensional effect very similar to Aran knitting but is much less complicated to work. A traditional Aran yarn should be used to work these stitches, which have a wide range of uses, including fashion and household designs.

Crochet rib stitch
This stitch is worked from side edge to side edge and requires sufficient chains to give the depth of ribbing. Make any number of chain.

1st row (RS) Into 3rd ch from hook work 1dc, 1dc into each ch to end. Turn.
2nd row 1ch to count as first dc, miss first dc, *work 1dc into horizontal loop below top loop of next dc, rep from * ending with 1dc into turning ch. Turn.
The 2nd row forms the pattern.

Crochet moss stitch
Make a number of chain divisible by 2 plus one extra chain.
1st row (RS) Into 3rd ch from hook work 1ss, *1htr into next ch, 1ss into next ch, rep from* to end. Turn.
2nd row 2ch to count as first htr, miss first ss, *1ss into next htr, 1htr into next ss, rep from * to end, 1ss into 2nd of first 2ch. Turn.
The 2nd row forms the pattern.

Crochet cluster stitch in panels
Make a number of chain divisible by 6 plus 4 and 1 extra chain, e.g. 29ch.
Base row (RS) Into 3rd ch from hook work 1dc, 1dc into each ch to end. Turn. 28 sts.
1st row 3ch to count as first tr, miss first dc, 1tr into each of next 3dc, *(yrh, insert hook into next dc and draw loop through very loosely) 4 times into same dc, yrh and draw through all 9 loops on hook—called 1Cl or cluster—, 1Cl into next dc, 1tr into each of next 4dc, rep from * to end. Turn.
2nd row 1ch to count as first dc, miss first tr, 1dc into each of next 3tr, *(work 1dc into next st inserting hook under st horizontally from front to back and round stem—called 1Fdc—) twice, 1dc into each of next 4tr, rep from * working last dc into 3rd of first 3ch. Turn.
3rd row 3ch to count as first tr, miss first dc, 1tr into each of next 3dc, *1Cl into each of next 2 sts, 1tr into each of next 4dc, rep from * working last tr into first ch. Turn.
The 2nd and 3rd rows form the pattern.

Crochet zig-zag stitch
Make a number of chain divisible by 8 plus 6 and 2 extra turning chain, e.g. 32ch.
Base row (RS) Into 4th ch from hook work 1tr, 1tr into each ch to end. Turn. 30 sts.
1st row 2ch, miss first tr, work 1tr round stem of next tr inserting hook from back to front—called RtB—, 1Rtb round each of next 3tr, *work 1tr round stem of next tr inserting hook from front to back—called RtF—, 1RtF round each of next 3tr, 1RtB round each of next 4tr, rep from * to end, 1tr into turning ch loop. Turn.
2nd row 2ch, miss first st, work 1RtF round each of next 4 sts, *work 1RtB round each of next 4 sts, 1RtF round each of next 4 sts, rep from * to end, 1tr into turning ch loop. Turn.
3rd row 2ch, miss first st, work 1RtF round next st, *work 1RtB round each of next 4 sts, 1RtF round each of next 4 sts, rep from * to last 4 sts, 1RtB round each of next 3 sts, 1tr into turning ch loop. Turn.
4th row 2ch, miss first st, work 1RtF round each of next 3 sts, *work 1Rtb round each of next 4 sts, 1RtF round each of next 4 sts, rep from * to last 2 sts, 1RtB round last st, 1tr into turning ch loop. Turn.
5th row 2ch, miss first st, work 1RtF round each of next 2 sts, *work 1RtB round each of next 4 sts, 1RtF round each of next 4 sts, rep from * to last 3 sts, 1RtB round each of next 2 sts, 1tr into turning ch loop. Turn.
6th row As 5th.
7th row As 4th.
8th row As 3rd.
9th row As 2nd.
10th row As 1st.
11th row As 4th.
12th row As 3rd.
13th row As 5th.
14th row As 5th.
15th row As 3rd.
16th row As 4th.
These 16 rows form the pattern.

Crochet Trinity stitch
Make a number of chain divisible by 2 plus 1 and 1 extra turning chain, e.g. 30ch.
Base row (RS) Into 3rd ch from hook work 1dc, 1dc into each ch to end. Turn. 29 sts.
1st row 1ch to count as edge st, *2ch, yrh, insert hook into next dc and draw a loop through loosely, yrh and draw through one loop on hook, (3 loops on hook), yrh, insert hook into same dc and draw a loop through loosely, (5 loops on hook), yrh and draw through 4 loops, yrh and draw through rem 2 loops—called B1—, 1ss into next dc, rep from * to last 2 sts, B1 into next dc, 1dc into 2nd of first 2ch. Turn.
2nd row 1ch to count as edge st, *1ss into next B1, 1dc into next ss, rep from * to last 2 sts, 1ss into B1, 1dc into first ch. Turn.
3rd row 1ch to count as edge st, *1ss into next ss, B1 into next dc, rep from * to last 2 sts, 1ss into next ss, 1dc into first ch. Turn.
4th row 1ch to count as edge st, *1dc into next ss, 1ss into next B1, rep from * to last 2 sts, 1dc into next ss, 1dc into first ch. Turn.
5th row 1ch to count as edge st, *B1 into next dc, 1ss into next ss, rep from * to last 2 sts, B1 into next dc, 1dc into first ch. Turn.
The 2nd to 5th rows form the pattern.

Surface crochet
Ridges of double crochet are worked on to the background fabric to form mock cables, or to enclose areas of patterned stitches, as shown in the diagrams.
To work surface crochet
Have the right side of the work facing you and join in the yarn with a slip stitch to the lower edge of the fabric. It is important to note that the yarn must be kept at the front of the work and if you hold it to the right of the stitch to be worked, the stitch leans slightly to the left and when the yarn is held to the left, the stitch leans slightly to the right. To work straight, vertical lines, either singly or in pairs, alternate the position of the yarn, first to the left and then to the right. To work diagonal lines, keep the yarn in the same direction as the slant stitch.

To work a straight surface line
Join the yarn and hold it on the RS of the work to the left of the hook, insert the hook under the first row to be worked and out to the front again, yrh and draw a loop through, yrh and draw through 2 loops on hook (one surface dc has been completed), hold the yarn at the right of the hook, insert the hook into the same hole at the top of the last surface dc, under the next row and out to the front again, yrh and draw a loop through, yrh and draw through 2 loops on hook. Continue in this way until the line is completed.

Rib pattern (worked across)

Moss stitch

Clusters in panels

Zig-zag pattern

Trinity stitch

Surface crochet

31

To work a diagonal surface line slanting to the left.
Join in the yarn and hold it on the RS of the work to the left of the hook, insert the hook under the first row to be worked and out to the front again, yrh and draw a loop through, yrh and draw through 2 loops on hook, (one surface dc has been completed), keep the yarn to the left of the hook, insert the hook one stitch to the left level with the top of the surface dc just completed and out to the front again, yrh and draw a loop through, yrh and draw through 2 loops on hook. Continue in this way until the line is completed.

To work a diagonal surface line slanting to the right
Work as given for diagonal line slanting to the left, keeping the yarn at the right of the hook and working each surface dc to the right.

In the diagrams given here, each square represents one stitch and one row of double crochet background. The single arrows indicate one line of surface crochet and the double arrows, 2 lines of surface crochet. Where the pattern lines converge, work both the lines into the same space. Where the lines intersect, cross the lines as indicated. The horizontal dotted lines indicate one pattern repeat.

Basic stitches

Reversible ridged double crochet
Make the required number of chain and one extra turning chain.
1st row (RS) Into 3rd ch from hook work 1dc, work 1dc into each ch to end.
2nd row 1ch to count as first dc, miss first dc, work 1dc into each dc to end working into back loop only of each dc of previous row, ending with 1dc into 2nd of first 2ch.
The 2nd row forms the pattern, ending with 1dc into first ch.

Reversible ridged half treble
Make the required number of chain and one extra turning chain.
1st row (RS) Into 3rd ch from hook work 1htr, work 1htr into each ch to end.
2nd row 2ch to count as first htr, miss first htr, work 1htr into each htr to end working into back loop only of each htr of previous row, ending with 1htr into 2nd of first 2ch.
The 2nd row forms the pattern.

Reversible ridged treble
Make the required number of chain and 2 extra turning chain.
1st row (RS) Into 4ch ch from hook work 1tr, work 1tr into each ch to end.
2nd row 3ch to count as first tr, miss first tr, work 1tr into each tr to end working into back loop only of each tr of previous row, ending with 1tr into 3rd of first 3ch.
The 2nd row forms the pattern.

Double treble
Make the required number of chain and 3 extra turning chain.
1st row (RS) Yrh twice, insert hook from front to back into 5th ch from hook, *yrh and draw loop through, (4 loops on hook), yrh and draw through 2 loops on hook, (3 loops on hook), yrh and draw through 2 loops on hook, (2 loops on hook), yrh and draw through rem 2 loops on hook, (1dtr has been made with the 4 missed ch counting as the turning ch), yrh twice, insert hook from front to back into next ch and rep from * working into each ch to end.
2nd row 4ch to count as first dtr, miss first dtr, work 1dtr into each dtr to end, ending with 1dtr into 4th of first 4ch.
The 2nd row forms the pattern.

Triple treble
Make the required number of chain and 4 extra turning chain.
1st row (RS) Yrh 3 times, insert hook from front to back into 6th ch from hook, *yrh and draw loop through, (5 loops on hook), yrh and draw through 2 loops, (4 loops on hook), yrh and draw through 2 loops on hook, (3 loops on hook), yrh and draw through 2 loops on hook, (2 loops on hook), yrh and draw through rem 2 loops on hook, (1tr tr has been made with the 5 missed ch counting as the turning ch), yrh 3 times, insert hook from front to back into next ch and rep from * working into each ch to end.
2nd row 5ch to count as first tr tr, miss first tr tr, work 1tr tr into each tr tr to end, ending with 1tr tr into 5th of first 5ch.
The 2nd row forms the pattern.

Eyelet treble
Make a number of chain divisible by 2 plus 1 and 2 extra turning chain.
1st row (RS) Into 4th ch from hook work 1tr, work 1tr into each ch to end.
2nd row 3ch to count as first tr, miss first tr, *1ch, miss 1tr, 1tr into next tr, rep from * to end, working last tr into 3rd of first 3ch.
3rd row 3ch to count as first tr, miss first tr, *1tr into 1ch, 1tr into next tr, rep from * to end, ending with 1tr into 1ch, 1tr into 3rd of first 3ch.
The 2nd and 3rd rows form the pattern.

Leaf stitch
Make a number of chain divisible by 2 and one extra turning chain.
1st row (RS) Into 3rd ch from hook work 2dc, *miss 1ch, work 2dc into next ch, rep from * to last 2ch, miss 1ch, 1dc into last ch.
2nd row 2ch to count as first st, miss first dc, *miss 1dc, work 2dc into next dc, rep from * to end, 1dc into turning ch.
The 2nd row forms the pattern.

Open treble
Make a number of chain divisible by 2 plus 1 and 2 extra turning chain.
1st row (RS) Into 5th ch from hook work 1tr, *1ch, miss 1ch, 1tr into next ch, rep from * to end.
2nd row 3ch to count as first tr, miss first tr, *1ch, 1tr into 1ch sp, rep from * to end.
The 2nd row forms the pattern.

Treble variation
Make the required number of chain and 2 extra turning chain.
1st row (RS) Into 4th ch from hook work 1tr, work 1tr into each ch to end.
2nd row 3ch to count as first tr, yrh, insert hook between first and 2nd tr and work 1tr, *yrh, insert hook between next 2tr and work 1tr, rep from * to end, ending with 1tr between last tr and first 3ch.
The 2nd row forms the pattern.

Reversible ridged double crochet

Reversible ridged half treble

Reversible ridged treble

Double treble

Triple treble

Eyelet treble

Leaf stitch

Open treble

Treble variation

33

Arch stitches

Mesh stitch
Make a number of chain divisible by 4 plus 1 and 5 extra turning chain.
1st row (RS) Into 10th ch from hook work 1dc, *5ch, miss 3ch, 1dc into next ch, rep from * to end.
2nd row 5ch, 1dc into 3rd ch of first 5ch loop, *5ch, 1dc into 3rd ch of next 5ch loop, rep from * to last loop, 5ch, 1dc into 6th of first 9ch, 2ch, miss 2ch, 1tr into next ch.
3rd row 6ch, *1dc into 3rd ch of next 5ch loop, 5ch, rep from * to end, 1dc into 3rd of first 5ch.
4th row 5ch, 1dc into 3rd ch of first 5ch loop, * 5ch, 1dc into 3rd ch of next loop, rep from * to last loop, 5ch, 1dc into 3rd ch of last loop, 2ch, 1tr into 1st of first 6ch.
The 3rd and 4th rows form the pattern.

Arch mesh stitch
Make a number of chain divisible by 4 plus 1 and 4 extra turning chain.
1st row (RS) Into 7th ch from hook work 1dc, 2ch, miss 1ch, 1tr into next ch, *2ch, miss 1ch, 1dc into next ch, 2ch, miss 1ch, 1tr into next ch, rep from * to end.
2nd row 1ch to count as first dc, miss first tr, *2ch, 1tr into next dc, 2ch, 1dc into next tr, rep from * to end, working the last dc into 4th of first 6ch.
3rd row 3ch to count as first tr, miss first dc, *2ch, 1dc into next tr, 2ch, 1tr into next dc, rep from * to end, working last tr into first 1ch.
4th row As 2nd row but working last dc into 3rd of first 3ch.
The 3rd and 4th rows form the pattern.

Zig-zag mesh stitch
Make a number of chain divisible by 4 plus 1 and 4 extra turning chain.
1st row (RS) Into 7th ch from hook work 1dc, 2ch, miss 1ch, 1tr into next ch, *2ch, miss 1ch, 1dc into next ch, 2ch, miss 1ch, 1tr into next ch, rep from * to end.
2nd row 1ch to count as first dc, miss first tr, *3ch, 1dc into next tr, rep from * to end, working last dc into 4th of first 6ch.
3rd row 3ch to count as first tr, *2ch, 1dc into 2nd of next 3ch, 2ch, 1tr into next dc, rep from * to end, working last tr into first 1ch.
4th row As 2nd row but working last dc into 3rd of first 3ch.
The 3rd and 4th rows form the pattern.

Picot mesh stitch
Make a number of chain divisible by 4 plus 1 and 5 extra turning chain.
1st row (RS) Into 10th ch from hook work 1dc, 3ch, 1dc into same ch as before, *5ch, miss 3ch, (1dc, 3ch, 1dc) into next ch —called 1 picot—, rep from * to last 4ch, 5ch, miss 3ch, 1dc into last ch.
2nd row 5ch, 1 picot into 3rd of first 5ch loop, *5ch, 1 picot into 3rd ch of next loop, rep from * to last loop, 5ch, 1 picot into 6th of first 9ch, 2ch, miss 2ch, 1tr into next ch.
3rd row 6ch, *1 picot into 3rd ch of next 5ch loop, 5ch, rep from * to last loop, 1 picot into last loop, 5ch, 1dc into 3rd of first 5ch.
4th row As 2nd row but ending with 5ch, 1 picot into 4th ch of last 6ch loop, 2ch, 1tr into first 1ch.
The 3rd and 4th rows form the pattern.

Fancy grill
Make a number of chain divisible by 4 plus 1 and 5 extra turning chain.
1st row (RS) Into 10th ch from hook work 1tr, *3ch, miss 3ch, 1tr into next ch, rep from * to end.
2nd row 3ch to count as first tr, miss first tr, *2ch, 1dc into 2nd of 3ch, 2ch, 1tr into next tr, rep from * to end, ending with 2ch, 1dc into 7th of first 9ch, 2ch, miss 1ch, 1tr into next ch.
3rd row 3ch to count as first tr, *3ch, 1tr into next tr, rep from * to end, working last tr into 3rd of first 3ch.
4th row As 2nd row but ending with 1dc into 2nd of 3ch, 2ch, 1tr into 3rd of first 3ch.
The 3rd and 4th rows form the pattern.

Mesh and clusters
Make a number of chain divisible by 8 plus 5 and 4 extra turning chain.
1st row (RS) Into 7th ch from hook work 1dc, *5ch, miss 3ch, 1dc into next ch, rep from * to last 2ch, 2ch, miss 1ch, 1tr into last ch.
2nd row 5ch, 1dc into first 5ch loop, *4ch, **yrh, insert hook into next loop, yrh and draw a loop through, yrh and draw through 2 loops on hook (2 loops now rem on hook), rep from ** 3 times more into same loop, noting that there will be one more loop on hook at end of each rep, (5 loops now on hook), yrh and draw through all loops on hook—called 1Cl —, 4ch, 1dc into next loop, rep from * to end, ending with 1dc into last 5ch loop, 2ch, 1tr into 4th of first 6ch.
3rd row 3ch, 1dc into 2ch loop, 5ch, *1dc into next 4ch loop, 5ch, rep from * to last loop, 1dc into last loop, 2ch, 1tr into first of first 5ch.
4th row 5ch, *1Cl into next 5ch loop, 4ch, 1dc into next 5ch loop, 4ch, rep from * to last 5ch loop, 1Cl into last 5ch loop, 2ch, 1tr into 3ch loop.
5th row As 3rd.
6th row As 2nd but ending with 1dc into last 5ch loop, 2ch, 1tr into 3ch loop.
The 3rd to 6th rows form the pattern.

Open V mesh
Make a number of chain divisible by 6 plus 1 and 3 extra turning chain.
1st row (RS) Into 7th ch from hook work (1tr, 2ch, 1tr)—called 1V—, *3ch, miss 2ch, 1dc into next ch, 3ch, miss 2ch, 1V into next ch, rep from * to last 3ch, 3ch, miss 2ch, 1dc into last ch.
2nd row 6ch, *1dc into 2ch sp of V, 3ch, 1tr into next dc, 3ch, rep from * to last V, 1dc into 2ch sp of V, 3ch, 1tr into 4th of first 6ch.
3rd row 4ch, *1V into next dc, 3ch, 1dc into next tr, 3ch, rep from * to end, ending with 1V into last dc, 3ch, 1dc into 3rd of first 6ch.
4th row As 2nd but ending with 1tr into first of first 4ch.
The 3rd and 4th rows form the pattern.

Straight mesh
Make a number of chain divisible by 6 plus 1 and 5 extra turning chain.
1st row (RS) Into 12th ch from hook work (1dc, 1ch, 1dc)—called 1V—, *5ch, miss 5ch, 1V into next ch, rep from * to last 6ch, 5ch, miss 5ch, 1dc into last ch.
2nd row 6ch, *1V into 1ch sp of V, 5ch, rep from * to end, ending with 1V into 1ch sp of V, 5ch, 1dc into 6th of first 11ch.
3rd row As 2nd but ending with 1dc into first of first 6ch.
The 3rd row forms the pattern.

Solomon's knot
There is no foundation chain for this stitch, which begins with a slip loop on the hook, 1ch.
1st row *Draw the loop on the hook up to 1.5cm ($\frac{1}{2}$in), yrh and draw a loop through, insert hook into the back loop only of the loop just made, yrh and draw a loop through, (2 loops now on hook), yrh and draw through 2 loops on hook—one knot has been made—, rep from * for required length, making an even number of knots.
2nd row Miss the knot on the hook and the next 3 knots, insert hook into centre of next knot and work 1dc, *make 2 knots, miss 1 knot along first row, 1dc into next knot, rep from * to end, working last dc into first ch at beg of first row.
3rd row Make 3 knots, 1dc into next unjoined knot of last row, *make 2 knots, 1dc into next unjoined knot of last row, rep from * to end.
The 3rd row forms the pattern.

Solomon's knot

Mesh stitch

Arch mesh stitch

Zig-zag mesh stitch

Picot mesh stitch

Fancy grill

Mesh and clusters

Open V mesh

Straight mesh

Solomon's knot

Shell stitches

Plain shell
Make a number of chain divisible by 6 plus 1.
1st row (RS) Into 4th ch from hook work 5tr, *miss 2ch, 1dc into next ch, miss 2ch, 5tr into next ch, rep from * to last 3ch, miss 2ch,

1dc into last ch.
2nd row 3ch to count as first tr, 2tr into first dc (edge st), *1dc into 3rd of 5tr, 5tr into next dc, rep from * to last shell, 1dc into 3rd of 5tr, 3tr into 3rd of first 3ch.

3rd row 1ch to count as first dc, *5tr into next dc, 1dc into 3rd of 5tr, rep from * to end working last dc into 3rd of first 3ch.
4th row As 2nd, working last 3tr into first 1ch.
The 3rd and 4th rows form the pattern.

Spaced shell
Make a number of chain divisible by 6 plus 1.
1st row (RS) Into 4th ch from hook work 5tr, *miss 2ch, 1dc into next ch, miss 2ch, 5tr into next ch, rep from * to last 3ch, miss 2ch, 1dc

into last ch.
2nd row 3ch to count as first tr, *2ch, 1dc into 3rd of 5tr, 2ch, 1tr into next dc, rep from * to last shell, 2ch, 1dc into 3rd of 5tr, 2ch, 1tr into 3rd of first 3ch.

3rd row 1ch to count as first dc, *5tr into next dc, 1dc into next tr, rep from * to end working last dc into 3rd of first 3ch.
4th row As 2nd, working last tr into first ch.
The 3rd and 4th rows form the pattern.

Open work shell
Make a number of chain divisible by 9 plus 1 and 4 extra turning chain.
1st row (WS) Into 8th ch from hook work 1dc, 3ch, miss 2ch, 1dc into next ch, 2ch, miss 2ch, 1tr into next ch, *2ch, miss 2ch, 1dc into next ch, 3ch, miss 2ch, 1dc into next ch,

2ch, miss 2ch, 1tr into next ch, rep from * to end.
2nd row 1ch to count as first dc, *1ch, miss 2ch sp, work (2tr, 1ch, 2tr, 1ch, 2tr) into 3ch sp, 1ch, miss 2ch sp, 1dc into next tr, rep from * to end working last dc into 5th of first 7ch.
3rd row 3ch to count as first tr, *2ch, 1dc into

1ch sp between first 2 pairs of tr, 3ch, 1dc into 1ch sp between next 2 pairs of tr, 2ch, 1tr into next dc, rep from * to end working last tr into first ch.
4th row As 2nd, working last dc into 3rd of first 3ch.
The 3rd and 4th rows form the pattern.

Open work double treble shell
Make a number of chain divisible by 8 plus 1 and 4 extra turning chain.
1st row (WS) Into 5th ch from hook work 1tr, *miss 3ch, work (1tr, 3ch, 1tr) into next ch, miss 3ch, work (1tr, 1ch, 1tr) into next ch, rep

from * to end.
2nd row 3ch to count as first tr, 1ch, 1tr into first 1ch sp, *6dtr into 3ch sp, work (1tr, 1ch, 1tr) into 1ch sp, rep from * to end working last (1tr, 1ch, 1tr) into sp between the turning ch and first tr.

3rd row 3ch to count as first tr, 1ch, 1tr into 1ch sp, *work (1tr, 3ch, 1tr) between 3rd and 4th of 6dtr, work (1tr, 1ch, 1tr) into 1ch sp, rep from * to end working last (1tr, 1ch, 1tr) into 1ch sp between the turning ch and first tr.
The 2nd and 3rd rows form the pattern.

Openwork spaced shell
Make a number of chain divisible by 10 plus 1 and 5 extra turning chain.
1st row (RS) Into 6th ch from hook work 1tr, *3ch, miss 3ch, 1dc into each of next 3ch, 3ch, miss 3ch, work (1tr, 3ch, 1tr) into next ch, rep from * to end, ending with (1tr, 2ch, 1tr) into last ch.
2nd row 3ch to count as first tr, 3tr into first 2ch sp, *3ch, 1dc into 2nd of 3dc, 3ch, 7tr into next 3ch sp between tr, rep from * to end, ending with 4tr into sp between turning ch and

first tr.
3rd row 1ch to count as first dc, 1dc into each of next 3tr, *5ch, 1dc into each of next 7tr, rep from * to last shell, 5ch, 1dc into each of next 3tr, 1dc into 3rd of first 3ch.
4th row 1ch to count as first dc, 1dc into next dc, *3ch, work (1tr, 3ch, 1tr) into 3rd of 5ch, 3ch, miss 2dc, 1dc into each of next 3dc, rep from * to end, ending with miss 2dc, 1dc into next dc, 1dc into first ch.
5th row 1ch to count as first dc, *3ch, 7tr into 3ch sp between tr, 3ch, 1dc into 2nd of 3dc,

rep from * to end working last dc into first ch.
6th row 1ch to count as first dc, 2ch, *1dc into each of next 7tr, 5ch, rep from * to last shell, 1dc into each of next 7tr, 2ch, 1dc into first ch.
7th row 3ch to count as first tr, 2ch, 1tr into first dc (edge st), *3ch, miss 2dc, 1dc into each of next 3dc, 3ch, work (1tr, 3ch, 1tr) into 3rd of 5ch, rep from * to end, ending with (1tr, 2ch, 1tr) into first ch.
The 2nd to 7th rows form the pattern.

Large shell
Make a number of chain divisible by 10 plus 1 and 1 extra turning chain.
1st row (RS) Into 3rd ch from hook work 1dc, *2ch, miss 3ch, 5tr into next ch, 2ch, miss 3ch, 1dc into each of next 3ch, rep from * to end, ending with 2dc instead of 3dc.
2nd row 1ch to count as first dc, *2ch, 1tr into first tr, (2tr into next tr, 1tr into next tr) twice, 2ch, miss 1dc, 1dc into next dc, rep from * to end working last dc into turning ch.

3rd row 3ch to count as first tr, *yrh, insert hook into first tr and draw a loop through, yrh and draw through 2 loops on hook, rep from * twice into same tr, (4 loops on hook), yrh and draw through all 4 loops on hook—called 3tr tog—, (2ch, miss 1tr, 3tr tog into next tr) 3 times, rep from * to end, 1tr into first ch.
4th row 1ch to count as first dc, 2ch, *1dc into next 2ch sp, 3ch, work (1dc, 3ch, 1dc) into next 2ch sp, 3ch, 1dc into next 2ch sp, 3ch, rep from * to end, omitting last 3ch and ending with 2ch,

1dc into 3rd of first 3ch.
5th row 1ch to count as first dc, 1dc into first 2ch sp, *2ch, miss next 3ch sp, 5tr into next 3ch sp, 2ch, miss next 3ch sp, 1dc into each of next 3ch, rep from * to end, omitting last 3dc and ending with 1dc into last 2ch sp, 1dc into first ch.
The 2nd to 5th rows form the pattern.

Off-centre shell
Make a number of chain divisible by 6 plus 1 and 1 extra turning chain.
1st row (RS) Into 5th ch from hook work (1tr, 2ch, 2tr), *1ch, miss 2ch, 1dc into next ch, 1ch, miss 2ch, work (1tr, 2ch, 2tr) into next ch, rep from * to last 3ch, 1ch, miss 2ch, 1dc into last ch.

2nd row 4ch, 2tr into first dc (edge st), *1ch, 1dc into 2ch sp, 1ch, work (1tr, 2ch, 2tr) into next dc, rep from * to end working last (1tr, 2ch, 2tr) into 3rd of first 4ch.
3rd row Ss into 2ch sp, 1ch to count as first dc, *1ch, work (1tr, 2ch, 2tr) into next dc, 1ch,

1dc into next 2ch sp, rep from * to end working last dc into the loop of turning ch.
4th row As 2nd, working last (1tr, 2ch, 2tr) into first ch.
The 3rd and 4th rows form the pattern.

Shell pattern in panels
Make a number of chain divisible by 13 plus 2 and 2 extra turning chain.
1st row (RS) Into 4th ch from hook work 1tr, 1tr into each ch to end.
2nd row 3ch to count as first tr, 1tr into each of next 3tr, *3ch, miss 3tr, 1dc into next tr, 3ch,

miss 3tr, 1tr into each of next 6tr, rep from * to end, ending with 1tr into each of next 3tr, 1tr into 3rd of first 3ch.
3rd row 3ch to count as first tr, 1tr into each of next 3tr, *1ch, 1dc into next 3ch sp, 3ch, 1dc into next 3ch sp, 1ch, 1tr into each of next 6tr, rep from * to end, ending with 1tr into each of

next 3tr, 1tr into 3rd of first 3ch.
4th row 3ch to count as first tr, 1tr into each of next 3tr, *7tr into 3ch sp, 1tr into each of next 6tr, rep from * to end, ending as given for previous rows.
The 2nd to 4th rows form the pattern.

Ribbon pattern
Make a number of chain divisible by 10 plus 1 and 2 extra turning chain.
1st row (RS) Into 4th ch from hook work 1tr, *3ch, miss 3ch, work (2tr, 2ch, 2tr) into next ch, 3ch, miss 3ch, 1tr into each of next 3ch, rep

from * to end, ending with 1tr into each of last 2ch.
2nd row 3ch to count as first tr, 1tr into next tr, *3ch, work (2tr, 2ch, 2tr) into 2ch sp, 3ch, 1tr into each of next 3tr, rep from * to end,

ending with 1tr into next tr, 1tr into 3rd of first 3ch.
The 2nd row forms the pattern.

Plain shell

Spaced shell

Openwork shell

Openwork double treble shell

Openwork spaced shell

Large shell

Off-centre shell

Shell pattern in panels

Ribbon pattern

Bobble & cluster stitches

Long bobble stitch

Make a number of chain divisible by 4 plus 1 and 1 extra turning chain.

1st row (RS) Into 3rd ch from hook work 1dc, 1dc into each ch to end.

2nd row 1ch to count as first dc, 1dc into next dc, *(yrh, insert hook into next dc and draw up a loop, yrh and draw through 2 loops on hook) 5 times into same dc, yrh and draw through all 6 loops on hook—called Mb or make bobble—, 1dc into each of next 3dc, rep from * to last 3dc, Mb into next dc, 1dc into next dc, 1dc into 2nd of first 2ch.

3rd row 1ch to count as first dc, 1dc into each st to end working last dc into first ch.

4th row 1ch to count as first dc, *1dc into each of next 3dc, Mb into next dc, rep from * to last 4 sts, 1dc into each of next 3dc, 1dc into first ch.

5th row As 3rd.

6th row As 2nd, ending with 1dc into first ch. The 3rd to 6th rows form the pattern. Different effects can be obtained by working more rows between each bobble row, noting that it must always be an odd number of rows, such as 3, 5, etc.

Short bobble stitch

Make a number of chain divisible by 4 plus 1 and 1 extra turning chain.

1st row (RS) Into 3rd ch from hook work 1dc, 1dc into each ch to end.

2nd row 1ch to count as first dc, 1dc into next dc, *(yrh, insert hook into next st and draw up a loop) 5 times into same dc, yrh and draw through 10 loops on hook, yrh and draw through rem 2 loops on hook—called Mb or make bobble—, 1dc into each of next 3dc, rep from * to last 3dc, Mb into next dc, 1dc into next dc, 1dc into 2nd of first 2ch.

3rd row 1ch to count as first dc, 1dc into each st to end working last dc into first ch.

4th row 1ch to count as first dc, *1dc into each of next 3dc, Mb into next dc, rep from * to last 4 sts, 1dc into each of next 3dc, 1dc into first ch.

5th row As 3rd.

6th row As 2nd, ending with 1dc into first ch. The 3rd to 6th rows form the pattern. The number of rows between bobble rows may be varied as given for long bobble stitch.

Raised bobble stitch

Make a number of chain divisible by 4 plus 1 and 1 extra turning chain.

1st row (RS) Into 3rd ch from hook work 1dc, 1dc into each ch to end.

2nd row 1ch to count as first dc, 1dc into each dc to end, ending with 1dc into 2nd of first 2ch.

3rd row 1ch to count as first dc, 1dc into next dc, *work 5tr into the st below the next dc 1 row down, take hook out of the working loop, insert hook from front to back under the top loop of the first of these 5tr, insert hook into the working loop and draw it through, 1ch, miss next dc noting that this st is the one worked into the row below—called Mb or make bobble—, 1dc into each of next 3dc, rep from * to last 3dc, Mb into st below next dc, 1dc into next dc, 1dc into first ch.

4th row 1ch to count as first dc, 1dc into each st to end missing each 1ch, working last dc into first ch.

5th row 1ch to count as first dc, *1dc into each of next 3dc, Mb into st below next dc, rep from

* to last 4 sts, 1dc into each of next 3dc, 1dc into first ch.

6th row As 4th. The 3rd to 6th rows form the pattern.

Bobbles forming a diamond pattern

The bobble in this pattern can be made by either the long or short bobble method. Make a number of chain divisible by 12 plus 3 and 1 extra turning chain.

1st row (RS) Into 3rd ch from hook work 1dc, 1dc into each ch to end.

2nd row 1ch to count as first dc, *Mb into next dc, 1dc into each of next 11dc, rep from * to last 2dc, Mb into next dc, 1dc into 2nd of first 2ch.

3rd and every alt row 1ch to count as first dc, 1dc into each st to end working last dc into first ch.

4th row 1ch to count as first dc, 1dc into each of next 2dc, *Mb into next dc, 1dc into each of next 7dc, Mb into next dc, 1dc into each of next 3dc, rep from * to end, ending with 1dc into each of next 2dc, 1dc into first ch.

6th row 1ch to count as first dc, *Mb into next dc, 1dc into each of next 3dc, rep from * to last 2 sts, Mb into next dc, 1dc into first ch.

8th row As 4th.

10th row As 2nd.

12th row 1ch to count as first dc, 1dc into each of next 5dc, *Mb into next dc, 1dc into each of next 11dc, rep from * to last 8 sts, Mb into next dc, 1dc into each of next 6dc, 1dc into first ch.

14th row 1ch to count as first dc, 1dc into each of next 4dc, *Mb into next dc, 1dc into each of next 3dc, Mb into next dc, 1dc into each of next 7dc, rep from * to last 10 sts, Mb into next dc, 1dc into each of next 3dc, Mb into next dc, 1dc into each of next 4dc, 1dc into first ch.

16th row 1ch to count as first dc, 1dc into each of next 2dc, *Mb into next dc, 1dc into each of next 3dc, rep from * to end, ending with 1dc into each of next 2dc, 1dc into first ch.

18th row As 14th.

20th row As 12th.

21st row As 3rd.

The 2nd to 21st rows form the pattern.

Shuttle stitch

Make a number of chain divisible by 4 plus 3 and 2 extra turning chain.

1st row (RS) Into 4th ch from hook work 1tr, 1tr into each ch to end.

2nd row 1ch to count as first dc, 1dc into each tr to end working last dc into 3rd of first 3ch.

3rd row 3ch to count as first tr, 1tr into each of next 2dc, *(yrh, insert hook from right to left behind the next st one row below, yrh and draw a loop through drawing it up to the same height as the tr on the row being worked) twice into the same st, (5 loops on hook), yrh and draw through 4 loops on hook, yrh and draw through rem 2 loops on hook, miss next dc noting that this st is the one worked into the row below—called Cl or cluster—, 1tr into each of next 3dc, rep from * to end, ending with 1tr into each of next 2dc, 1tr into first ch.

4th row 1ch to count as first dc, 1dc into each st to end working last dc into 3rd of first 3ch.

5th row 3ch to count as first tr, *Cl into st below next dc (the tr on 3rd row), 1tr into each of next 3dc, rep from * to last 2 sts, Cl into st below next dc, 1tr into first ch.

6th row As 4th. The 3rd to 6th rows form the pattern.

Pineapple stitch

Make a number of chain divisible by 3 plus 2 and 1 extra turning chain.

1st row (RS) Into 3rd ch from hook work 1dc, 1dc into each ch to end.

2nd row 1ch, 1dc into first dc (edge st), 1ch, draw this ch up to 1.5cm ($\frac{1}{2}$in), (yrh, insert hook into the vertical loop of the dc, yrh and draw a loop through drawing it up to 1.5cm ($\frac{1}{2}$in)) 4 times into same place, miss 2dc, insert hook from front to back into the next dc, yrh and draw loop through the dc and all 9 loops on hook—called Cl or cluster—, *2ch, draw the 2nd ch up to 1.5cm ($\frac{1}{2}$in), (yrh, insert hook into the vertical loop at the side of the last Cl, yrh and draw loop through drawing it up to 1.5cm ($\frac{1}{2}$in)) 4 times into same place, miss 2dc, insert hook into next dc and complete Cl as before, rep from * ending with 1ch, 1tr into 2nd of first 2ch.

3rd row 3ch to count as first tr, work 3tr into each Cl to end, inserting the hook under the top 2 loops of each Cl, ending with 1tr into first ch.

4th row 1ch, 1dc into first tr (edge st), work Cl to end as given for 2nd row but miss 2tr instead of 2dc, ending with 1tr into 3rd of first 3ch. The 3rd and 4th rows form the pattern.

Double treble cluster stitch

Make a number of chain divisible by 4 plus 1 and 1 extra turning chain.

1st row (RS) Into 3rd ch from hook work 1dc, 1dc into each ch to end.

2nd row 4ch to count as first dtr, 1dtr into first dc (edge st), *miss 3dc, 4dtr into next dc, rep from * to last 4dc, miss 3dc, 2dtr into 2nd of first 2ch.

3rd row 1ch to count as first dc, *4ch, work 1dc between 2nd and 3rd dtr of next gr of 4dtr, rep from * to end, ending with 4ch, 1dc into 4th of first 4ch.

4th row 4ch to count as first dtr, 1dtr into first dc (edge st), *4dtr into next dc, rep from * to end, ending with 2dtr into first ch. The 3rd and 4th rows form the pattern.

Long bobble stitch

Short bobble stitch

Raised bobble stitch

Bobbles forming a diamond pattern

Shuttle stitch

Pineapple stitch

Double treble cluster stitch

Bell cluster stitch

Daisy stitch

Bell cluster stitch
Make a number of chain divisible by 4 plus 2 and 1 extra turning chain.

1st row (RS) Into 3rd ch from hook work 1dc, 1dc into each ch to end.

2nd row 4ch to count as first dtr, 2ch, *keeping the last loop of each st on hook work 1dtr into each of next 4dc, yrh and draw through all 5 loops on hook—called Cl or cluster—, 4ch, rep from * to last 5dc, work Cl over next 4dc, 2ch, 1dtr into 2nd of first 2ch.

3rd row 1ch to count as first dc, 1dc into each of next 2ch, *miss Cl, 1dc into each of next 4ch, rep from * to end, ending with miss Cl, 1dc into each of next 2ch, 1dc into 4th of first 4ch.

4th row As 2nd, working last dtr into first ch. The 3rd and 4th rows form the pattern.

Daisy stitch
Make a number of chain divisible by 2 plus 1 and 4 extra turning chain.

1st row (RS) Insert hook into 2nd ch from hook, yrh and draw a loop through, (insert hook into next ch, yrh and draw a loop through) 4 times, yrh and draw through all 6 loops on hook, 1ch, *insert hook into hole at top of daisy just made, yrh and draw a loop through, insert hook into back of last loop of same daisy, yrh and draw a loop through, insert hook into same ch as last loop of same daisy, yrh and draw a loop through, (insert hook into next ch, yrh and draw a loop through) twice, yrh and draw through all 6 loops on hook, 1ch, rep from * to last ch, 1dc into last ch.

2nd row 2ch, 1dc into hole of first daisy, *1ch, 1dc into hole of next daisy, rep from * to end, 1dc into first ch.

3rd row 3ch, insert hook into 2nd ch from hook, yrh and draw a loop through, insert hook into next ch, yrh and draw a loop through, insert hook into next dc, yrh and draw a loop through, insert hook into next dc, yrh and draw a loop through, insert hook into 1ch sp, yrh and draw a loop through, yrh and draw through all 6 loops on hook, 1ch, *insert hook into hole at top of daisy just made, yrh and draw a loop through, insert hook into back of last loop of same daisy, yrh and draw a loop through, insert hook into same 1ch sp as before, yrh and draw a loop through, insert hook into next dc, yrh and draw a loop through, insert hook into next 1ch sp, yrh and draw a loop through, yrh and draw through all 6 loops on hook, 1ch, rep from * to end, 1dc into first 1ch.
The 2nd and 3rd rows form the pattern.

Large patterns

Basket stitch
Make a number of chain divisible by 10 plus 7 and 2 extra turning chain.

1st row (RS) Into 4th ch from hook work 1tr, 1tr into each ch to end.

2nd row 3ch to count as first tr, yrh, insert hook from the back round stem of next tr, yrh and draw loop through, yrh and draw through 2 loops, yrh and draw through rem 2 loops—called RtB or raised treble from the back, see diagram B—, 1RtB round each of next 4tr, *1tr into each of next 5tr, 1RtB round each of next 5tr, rep from * to last st, 1tr into 3rd of first 3ch.

3rd row 3ch to count as first tr, yrh, insert hook from the front round stem of next tr, yrh and draw loop through, yrh and draw through 2 loops, yrh and draw through rem 2 loops—called RtF or raised treble from the front, see diagram A—, 1RtF round each of next 4tr, *1tr into each of next 5tr, 1RtF round each of next 5tr, rep from * to last st, 1tr into 3rd of first 3ch.

4th row As 2nd.

5th row 3ch to count as first tr, 1tr into each of next 5tr, *1RtF round each of next 5tr, 1tr into each of next 5tr, rep from * to last st, 1tr into 3rd of first 3ch.

6th row 3ch to count as first tr, 1tr into each of next 5tr, *1RtB round each of next 5tr, 1tr into each of next 5tr, rep from * to last st, 1tr into 3rd of first 3ch.

7th row As 5th.

8th row As 6th.

9th row As 3rd.

10th row As 2nd.
The 3rd to 10th rows form the pattern.

Open work squares
Make a number of chain divisible by 17 plus 2 and 2 extra turning chain

1st row (RS) Into 4th ch from hook work 1tr, 1tr into each ch to end.

2nd row 3ch to count as first tr, 1tr into each tr to end working last tr into 3rd of first 3ch.

3rd row 3ch to count as first tr, 1tr into each of next 3tr, *3ch, miss 2tr, 1dc into next tr, (5ch, miss 2tr, 1dc into next tr) twice, 3ch, miss 2tr, 1tr into each of next 6tr, rep from * to end, ending with 1tr into each of next 3tr, 1tr into 3rd of first 3ch.

4th row 3ch to count as first tr, 1tr into each of next 3tr, *5ch, (yrh, insert hook into next

5ch loop and draw up a loop) 3 times, yrh and draw through all 7 loops on hook—called 1Cl or cluster—, 5ch, 1Cl into next 5ch loop, 5ch, 1tr into each of next 6tr, rep from * to end, ending as given for 3rd row.

5th row 3ch to count as first tr, 1tr into each of next 3tr, *3ch, (1Cl into next 5ch loop, 5ch) twice, 1Cl into next 5ch loop, 3ch, 1tr into each of next 6tr, rep from * to end, ending as given for 3rd row.

6th row 3ch to count as first tr, 1tr into each of next 3tr, *(5ch, 1Cl into next 5ch loop) twice, 5ch, 1tr into each of next 6tr, rep from * to end, ending as given for 3rd row.

7th row 3ch to count as first tr, 1tr into each of next 3tr, *3ch, (1dc into next 5ch loop, 5ch) twice, 1dc into next 5ch loop, 3ch, 1tr into each of next 6tr, rep from * to end, ending as given for 3rd row.

8th row 3ch to count as first tr, 1tr into each of next 3tr, *2tr into 3ch loop, 1tr into next dc, (2tr into 5ch loop, 1tr into next dc) twice, 2tr into 3ch loop, 1tr into each of next 6tr, rep from * to end, ending as given for 3rd row.
The 2nd and 8th rows form the pattern.

Open work butterflies
Make a number of chain divisible by 12 plus 1 and 1 extra turning chain.

1st row (RS) Into 3rd ch from hook work 1dc, 1dc into each ch to end.

2nd row 3ch to count as first tr, 3tr into first dc (edge st), *4ch, miss 4dc, 1dc into each of next 3dc, 4ch, miss 4dc, 7tr into next dc, rep from * to last 12 sts, 4ch, miss 4dc, 1dc into each of

next 3dc, 4ch, miss 4dc, 4tr into 2nd of first 2ch.

3rd row 2ch to count as first htr, 1htr into each of next 3tr, *4ch, 1dc into 2nd of 3dc, 4ch, 1htr into each of next 7tr, rep from * to end, ending with 1htr into each of next 3tr, 1htr into 3rd of first 3ch.

4th row 3ch to count as first tr, 1tr into each of next 3htr, *3tr into 4ch loop, 3tr into next 4ch loop, 1tr into each of next 7htr, rep from * to end, ending with 1tr into each of next 3htr, 1tr into 2nd of first 2ch.

5th row 1ch to count as first dc, 1dc into each of next 5tr, *3ch, miss 2tr, 1dc into each of next 11tr, rep from * to end, ending with 1dc into each of next 5tr, 1dc into 3rd of first 3ch.

6th row 3ch to count as first tr, 3tr into first dc (edge st), *4ch, miss 5dc, 1dc into each of of next 3ch, 4ch, miss 5dc, 7tr into next dc, rep from * to end, ending with 4tr into first ch.
The 3rd to 6th rows form the pattern.

Diamond pattern
Make a number of chain divisible by 14 plus 1 and 1 extra turning chain.

1st row (RS) Into 3rd ch from hook work 1dc, 1dc into next ch, *4ch, miss 3ch, 1tr into next ch, 2tr into next ch, 4ch, miss 3ch, 1dc into each of next 5ch, rep from * to end, ending with 1dc into each of last 3ch.

2nd row 1ch to count as first dc, 1dc into next dc, *3ch, 4tr into 4ch loop, 1ch, 4tr into next 4ch loop, 3ch, miss 1dc, 1dc into each of next 3dc, rep from * to end, ending with miss 1dc, 1dc into next dc, 1dc into 2nd of first 2ch.

3rd row 3ch to count as first tr, *3ch, 4tr into

Basket stitch

Openwork squares

Openwork butterflies

Diamond pattern

Large diamond pattern

Pyramid pattern

3ch sp, 3ch, 1dtr into single 1ch, 3ch, 4tr into next 3ch sp, 3ch, 1tr into 2nd of 3dc, rep from * to end working last tr into first ch.

4th row 3ch to count as first tr, *4tr into 3ch sp, 3ch, 1dc into next 3ch sp, 1dc into dtr, 1dc into next 3ch sp, 3ch, 4tr into next 3ch sp, 1ch, rep from * to end omitting last 1ch and ending with 1tr into 3rd of first 3ch.

5th row 3ch to count as first tr, 1tr into first tr (edge st), *4ch, 1dc into next 3ch sp, 1dc into each of next 3dc, 1dc into next 3ch sp, 4ch, 4tr into 1ch sp, rep from * to end, ending with 2tr into 3rd of first 3ch.

6th row 3ch to count as first tr, *4tr into 4ch sp, 3ch, miss 1dc into each of next 3dc, 3ch, 4tr into next 4ch sp, 1ch, rep from * to end, omitting last 1ch and ending with 1tr into 3rd of first 3ch.

7th row 4ch to count as first dtr, *3ch, 4tr into 3ch sp, 3ch, 1tr into 2nd of 3dc, 3ch, 4tr into next 3ch sp, 3ch, 1dtr into single 1ch, rep from * to end working last dtr into 3rd of first 3ch.

8th row 1ch to count as first dc, 1dc into 3ch sp, *3ch, 4tr into next 3ch sp, 1ch, 4tr into next 3ch sp, 3ch, 1dc into next 3ch sp, 1dc into dtr, 1dc into next 3ch sp, rep from * to end, ending with 1dc into 3ch sp, 1dc into 4th of first 4ch.

9th row 3ch to count as first tr, 1dc into next dc, *1dc into 3ch sp, 4ch, 4tr into 1ch sp, 4ch, 1dc into next 3ch sp, 1dc into each of next 3dc, rep from * to end, ending with 1dc into 3ch sp, 1dc into next dc, 1dc into first ch.
The 2nd to 9th rows form the pattern.

Large diamond pattern
Make a number of chain divisible by 15 plus 1 and 3 extra turning chain.
1st row (RS) Into 5th ch from hook work 1tr, 1tr into each of next 5ch, *2ch, miss 1ch, 1tr into each of next 6ch, 3ch, miss 2ch, 1tr into each of next 6ch, rep from * to last 9ch, 2ch, miss 1ch, 1tr into each of next 6ch, 1ch, miss 1ch, 1tr into last ch.

2nd row 2ch, noting that these and ch on subsequent rows do not count as a st, 1dc into 1ch sp, *3ch, miss 2tr, 1tr into each of next 4tr, 2ch, 1tr into each of next 4tr, 3ch, 1dc into 3ch sp, rep

from * to end working last dc into turning ch loop at beg of 1st row.

3rd row 4ch, 1dc into 3ch sp, *3ch, miss 2tr, 1tr into each of next 2tr, 2ch, 1tr into each of next 2tr, 1dc into 3ch sp, 3ch, 1dc into 3ch sp, rep from * to end working last dc into turning ch loop.

4th row 3ch, 1dc into first 3ch sp, *3ch, 1dc into next 3ch sp, 3ch, 2tr into 2ch sp, (3ch, 1dc into next 3ch sp) twice, rep from * to end working last dc into turning ch loop.

5th row 4ch, 1dc into first 3ch sp, *3ch, 2tr into next 3ch sp, 2ch, 2tr into next 3ch sp, (3ch, 1dc into next 3ch sp) twice, rep from * to end working last dc into turning ch loop.

6th row 3ch, 1dc into first 3ch sp, *3ch, 2tr into next 3ch sp, 1tr into each of next 2tr, 2ch, 1tr into each of next 2tr, 2tr into next 3ch sp, 3ch, 1dc into next 3ch sp, rep from * to end working last dc into turning ch loop.

7th row 4ch, *2tr into next 3ch sp, 1tr into each of next 4tr, 3ch, 1tr into each of next 4tr, 2tr into next 3ch sp, 2ch, rep from * to end omitting last 2ch and ending with 1ch, 1tr into turning ch loop.

8th row 4ch, *1tr into each of next 4tr, 3ch, 1dc into 3ch sp, 3ch, miss 2tr, 1tr into each of next 4tr, 2ch, rep from * to end omitting last 2ch and ending with 1ch, 1tr into turning ch loop.

9th row 4ch, *1tr into each of next 2tr, (3ch, 1dc into next 3ch sp) twice, 3ch, miss 2tr, 1tr into each of next 2tr, 2ch, rep from * to end omitting last 2ch and ending with 1ch, 1tr into turning ch loop.

10th row 3ch, 1tr into 1ch sp, *(3ch, 1dc into next 3ch sp) 3 times, 3ch, 2tr into 2ch sp, rep from * to end working last 2tr into turning ch loop.

11th row 4ch, *2tr into next 3ch sp, (3ch, 1dc into next 3ch sp) twice, 3ch, 2tr into next 3ch sp, 2ch, rep from * to end omitting last 2ch and ending with 1ch, 1tr into turning ch loop.

12th row 4ch, *1tr into each of next 2tr, 2tr into next 3ch sp, 3ch, 1dc into next 3ch sp, 3ch, 2tr into next 3ch sp, 1tr into each of next 2tr, 2ch, rep from * to end omitting last 2ch and ending with 1ch, 1tr into turning ch loop.

13th row 4ch, *1tr into each of next 4tr, 2tr into 3ch sp, 2ch, 2tr into next 3ch sp, 1tr into each of next 4tr, 3ch, rep from * to end omitting last 3ch and ending with 1ch, 1tr into turning ch loop.
The 2nd to 13th rows form the pattern.

Pyramid pattern
Make a number of chain divisible by 10 plus 1 and 3 extra turning chain.
1st row (WS) Into 4th ch from hook work 1tr, *4ch, miss 4ch, 1dc into next ch, 4ch, miss 4ch, 3tr into next ch, rep from * to end, ending with 2tr into last ch.

2nd row 3ch to count as first tr, *2tr into next tr, 3ch, 1dc into dc, 3ch, 2tr into next tr, 1tr into next tr, rep from * to end working last tr into 3rd of first 3ch.

3rd row 3ch to count as first tr, 1tr into next tr, *2tr into next tr, 2ch, 1dc into next dc, 2ch, 2tr into next tr, 1tr into each of next 3tr, rep from * to end, ending with 2tr into next tr, 1tr into next tr, 1tr into 3rd of first 3ch.

4th row 3ch to count as first tr, 1tr into each of next 2tr, *2tr into next tr, 1ch, 2tr into next tr, 1tr into each of next 5tr, rep from * to end, ending with 2tr into next tr, 1tr into each of next 2tr, 1tr into 3rd of first 3ch.

5th row 1ch to count as first dc, *4ch, 3tr into 1ch sp, 4ch, 1dc into 5th of 9tr, rep from * to end working last dc into 3rd of first 3ch.

6th row 1ch to count as first dc, *3ch, 2tr into next tr, 1tr into next tr, 2tr into next tr, 3ch, 1dc into next dc, rep from * to end working last dc into first ch.

7th row 1ch to count as first dc, *2ch, 2tr into next tr, 1tr into each of next 3tr, 2tr into next tr, 2ch, 1dc into next dc, rep from * to end working last dc into first ch.

8th row 3ch to count as first tr, 1ch, *2tr into next tr, 1tr into each of next 5tr, 2tr into next tr, 1ch, rep from * to end, 1tr into first ch.

9th row 3ch to count as first tr, 1tr into first tr (edge st), *4ch, 1dc into 5th of 9tr, 4ch, 3tr into 1ch sp, rep from * to end, ending with 2tr into 3rd of first 3ch.
The 2nd to 9th rows form the pattern.

His & hers crochet cardigan

Sizes
To fit 81.5 [86.5:91.5:96.5:101.5]cm (32[34:36:38:40]in) chest
Length to shoulder, 63.0 [64.0:65.0:66.0:67.0]cm (24¾[25¼:25½:26:26½]in)
Sleeve seam, 43.0[44.0:45.0:46.0:47.0]cm (17[17¼:17¾:18:18½]in)
The figures in brackets [] refer to the 86.5 (34), 91.5 (36), 96.5 (38) and 101.5cm (40in) sizes respectively
Tension
16 sts and 9 rows to 10cm (3.9in) over tr worked on No.4.50 (ISR) crochet hook
Materials
10[11:11:12:13] x 50grm balls Jaeger Spiral Spun Double Knitting
One No.4.50 (ISR) crochet hook
One No.4.00 (ISR) crochet hook
6 buttons

Back
Using No.4.50 (ISR) hook make 69[73:77:81:85] ch.
1st row Into 3rd ch from hook work 1dc, 1dc into each ch to end. Turn. 68[72:76:80:84] sts.
2nd row 3ch to count as first tr, 1tr into each dc to end. Turn.
Rep 2nd row 39 times more.
Shape armholes
Next row Ss across first 5 sts, patt to last 5 sts, turn.
Break off yarn and leave work for time being.

Left front
Using No.4.50 (ISR) hook make 34[36:38:40:42] ch.
Work first 2 rows as given for back. 33[35:37:39:41] sts. Rep 2nd row 39 times more, ending with a RS row.
Shape armhole

Next row Patt to last 5 sts, turn.
Break off yarn and leave for time being.

Right front
Using No.4.50 (ISR) hook make 34[36:38:40:42] ch.
Work 41 rows as given for left front.
Shape armhole
Next row Ss across first 5 sts, patt to end.
Do not break off yarn but leave for time being.

Back and fronts worked in one piece
Optional method
Using No.4.50 (ISR) hook make 135[143:151:159:167] ch. Work first 2 rows as given for back. 134[142:150:158:166] sts. Rep 2nd row 39 times more, ending with a RS row.
Divide for armholes
Next row 3ch to count as first tr, 1tr into each of next 27[29:31:33:35]tr, ss across next 10tr

to form underarm, 1tr into each of next 58[62:66:70:74] tr, ss across next 10tr to form 2nd underarm, 1tr into each of next 28[30:32:34:36] tr. Do not break off yarn but leave for time being.

Sleeves

Using No.4.50 (ISR) hook make 34[36:38:40:42] ch.
Work first 2[2:4:4:4] rows as given for back. 33[35:37:39:41] sts. Cont in patt as given for back, inc one st at each end of next and every foll 4th row until there are 51[53:55:57:59] sts. Cont without shaping until sleeve measures 43.0 [44.0:45.0:46.0:47.0]cm (17[17¼:17¾:18:18½]in) from beg, or required length to underarm ending with a RS row. Mark each end of last row with coloured thread. Work a further 3 rows, noting that these 3 rows are set into armhole shaping. Break off yarn and leave for time being.

Yoke

Using No.4.50 (ISR) hook and with RS of work facing, return to right front where yarn was left and work across all pieces as foll:-
1st row 3ch, 1tr into each of next 24[26:28:30:32] tr, yrh, insert hook into next st and draw up a loop, yrh and draw through 2 loops on hook, yrh, insert hook into next st and draw up a loop, yrh and draw through 2 loops on hook, yrh and draw through rem 3 loops on hook — called 2tr tog —, 1tr into next tr noting that this is the last tr of right front, cont across one sleeve, 1tr into first st, 2tr tog, 1tr into each of next 45[47:49:51:53] tr, 2tr tog, 1tr into next tr, cont across back, 1tr into first tr, 2tr tog, 1tr into each of next 52[56:60:64:68] tr, 2tr tog, 1tr into next tr, work across 2nd sleeve as given for first sleeve, cont across left front, 1tr into first tr, 2tr tog, 1tr into each tr to end. Turn. 208[:220:232:244:256] sts.
2nd row 3ch to count as first tr, 2tr tog, 1tr into each of next 21[23:25:27:29] tr, 2tr tog, 1tr into each of next 2tr, 2tr tog, 1tr into each of next 43[45:47:49:51] tr, 2tr tog, 1tr into each of next 2tr, 2tr tog, 1tr into each of next 50[54:58:62:66] tr, 2tr tog, 1tr into each of next 2tr, 2tr tog, 1tr into each of next 43[45:47:49:51] tr, 2tr tog, 1tr into each of next 2tr, 2tr tog, 1tr into each of next 21[23:25:27:29] tr, 2tr tog, 1tr into last st. Turn. 198[210:222:234:246] sts.
3rd row 3ch, work 21[23:25:27:29] tr, 2tr tog, 2tr, 2tr tog, 41[43:45:47:49] tr, 2tr tog, 2tr, 2tr tog, 48[52:56:60:64] tr, 2tr tog, 2tr, 2tr tog, 41[43:45:47:49] tr, 2tr tog, 2tr, 2tr tog, 22[24:26:28:30] tr. Turn.
4th row 3ch, 2tr tog, work 18[20:22:24:26] tr, 2tr tog, 2tr, 2tr tog, 39[41:43:45:47] tr, 2tr tog, 2tr, 2tr tog, 46[50:54:58:62] tr, 2tr tog, 2tr, 2tr tog, 39[41:43:45:47]tr, 2tr tog, 2tr, 2tr tog, 18[20:22:24:26] tr, 2tr tog, 1tr into last st. Turn.
5th row Work as given for 3rd row, allowing for sts dec and shaping each raglan seam by working 2tr tog, 2tr, 2tr tog. Turn.
6th row Work as given for 4th row, allowing for sts dec and dec as before at each raglan seam and at each end of row. Turn.
7th row as 5th. 154[166:178:190:202] sts.
8th row 3ch, 2tr tog, work 12[14:16:18:20] tr, 2tr tog, 2tr, 2tr tog, *across sleeve work 13[14:15:16:17] tr, 2tr tog, 1tr, 2tr tog, 13[14:15:16:17] tr, *, 2tr tog, 2tr, 2tr tog, work 38[42:46:50:54] tr, 2tr tog, 2tr, 2tr tog, rep from * to * across other sleeve, 2tr tog, 2tr, 2tr tog, work 12[14:16:18:20] tr, 2tr tog, 1tr into last st. Turn. 140[152:164:176:188] sts.
Mark 1tr between the dec at centre of each sleeve. Cont dec at front edges at each end of every alt row until 6[7:8:9:10] sts in all have been dec and dec at each side of centre marked st on each sleeve on every 3rd[3rd:3rd:4th:4th] row 3 times more, *at the same time* dec as before at each

raglan seam on every row until 36[38:40:42:44] sts rem. Fasten off.

Front band (for man)

Using No.4.00 (ISR) hook and with RS of work facing, rejoin yarn at lower edge of right front, work approx 3dc into every 2 rows up front edge, 1dc into each st across sleeve tops and back neck, then 3dc into every 2 rows down left front. Turn. Work 2 more rows dc.
4th row 1ch, 1dc into each of next 2dc, *2ch, miss 2dc, 1dc into each of next 9dc, rep from * 5 times more, work in dc to end. Turn.
5th row Work in dc to end, working 2dc into each 2ch buttonhole. Turn.

Work 2 more rows dc. Fasten off.

Front band (for woman)

Work first 3 rows as given for man.
4th row 1ch, 1dc into each dc to last 60dc, *2ch, miss 2dc, 1dc into each of next 9dc, rep from * 4 times more, 2ch, miss 2dc, 1dc into each of next 3dc. Turn.
Complete as given for front band for man.

To make up

Do not press. Sew last 3 rows of sleeve seams to cast off sts at underarm. Join side seams if worked separately. Join sleeve seams. Press seams under a damp cloth with a warm iron. Sew on buttons.

Miscellaneous patterns

Brick pattern
Make a number of chain divisible by 4 and 2 extra turning chain.
1st row (RS) Into 4th ch from hook work 1tr, 1tr into each ch to end.
2nd row 1ch to count as first dc, 3ch, miss next 3tr, 1dc between next 2tr *3ch, miss 4tr, 1dc between next 2tr, rep from * to end working last dc into 3rd of first 3ch.
3rd row Ss into first 3ch loop, 3ch to count as first tr, 3tr into same loop, *4tr into next 3ch loop, rep from * to last loop, 3tr into last loop, 1tr into first ch.
4th row 1ch to count as first dc, 1ch, miss 1tr, 1dc between next 2tr, *3ch, miss 4tr, 1dc between next 2tr, rep from * to last 2tr, 1ch, miss 1tr, 1dc into 3rd of first 3ch.
5th row Ss into 1ch sp, 3ch to count as first tr, 1tr into 1ch sp, *4tr into next 3ch loop, rep from * to end, ending with 1tr into 1ch sp, 1tr into first ch.
The 2nd to 5th rows form the pattern.

Brick pattern in panels
Make a number of chain divisible by 9 plus 2 and 2 extra turning chain.
1st row (RS) Into 4th ch from hook work 1tr, 1tr into each of next 2ch, *2ch, miss 1ch, 1dc into next ch, 2ch, miss 1ch, 1tr into each of next 6ch, rep from * to end, ending with 1tr into each of next 4ch.
2nd row Ss into sp between first 2tr, work 1dc into same sp, *(3ch, 1dc into next 2ch sp) twice, 3ch, 1dc between 3rd and 4th of next 6tr, rep from * to end working last dc between last tr and first 3ch.
3rd row 3ch to count as first tr, *3tr into next 3ch loop, 2ch, 1dc into next 3ch loop, 2ch, 3tr into next 3ch loop, rep from * to end, 1tr into last dc.
The 2nd and 3rd rows form the pattern.

Crazy pattern
Make a number of chain divisible by 4 plus 1 and 3 extra turning chain.
1st row (RS) Into 4th ch from hook work 3tr, *miss 3ch, work (1dc, 2ch, 3tr) into next ch, rep from * to last 4ch, miss 3ch, 1dc into last ch.
2nd row 3ch, 3tr into first dc (edge st), *work (1dc, 2ch, 3tr) into next 2ch sp, rep from * to last group, 1dc into 3rd of first 3ch.
The 2nd row forms the pattern. If a straight edge is required to complete this pattern, work the last row as foll:-
Last row 3ch, 1tr into first dc (edge st), *1ch, 1dc into 2ch sp, 2tr into next dc, rep from * to end, ending with 1dc into 3rd of first 3ch.

Florette pattern
Make a number of chain divisible by 3 plus 1 and 3 extra turning chain.
1st row (RS) Into 4th ch from hook work 2tr, *miss 2ch, 3tr into next ch, rep from * to end.
2nd row 1ch, *miss 2tr, 3dc into next tr, rep from * to last 3tr, miss 2tr, 1dc into 3rd of first 3ch.
3rd row 3ch to count as first tr, 2tr into first dc (edge st), *miss 2dc, 3tr into next dc, rep from * to end.
The 2nd and 3rd rows form the pattern.

Close fabric stitch
Make a number of chain divisible by 2 and 3 extra turning chain.
1st row (RS) Into 5th ch from hook work 1dc and 1tr, *miss 1ch, work (1dc and 1tr) into next ch, rep from * to last 2ch, miss 1ch, 1dc into last ch.
2nd row 3ch to count as first tr, *work (1dc and 1tr) into next dc, rep from * to end, 1dc into 4th of first 4ch.
3rd row As 2nd row but ending with 1dc into 3rd of first 3ch.
The 3rd row forms the pattern.

Forget-me-not stitch
Make a number of chain divisible by 3 plus 1 and 4 extra turning chain.
1st row (RS) Into 5th ch from hook work (2tr, 2ch, 1dc), *miss 2ch, work (2tr, 2ch, 1dc) into next ch, rep from * to last 3ch, miss 2ch, 1dc into last ch.
2nd row 3ch to count as first tr, *into next 2ch sp work (2tr, 2ch, 1dc), rep from * to end, 1dc into 4th of first 4ch.
3rd row As 2nd but ending with 1dc into 3rd of first 3ch.
The 3rd row forms the pattern.

Spaced treble groups
Make a number of chain divisible by 2 plus 1 and 2 extra turning chain.
1st row (RS) Into 4th ch from hook work 1tr, 1tr into each ch to end.
2nd row 3ch to count as first tr, 1ch, yrh, insert hook into next tr and draw a loop through, yrh and draw through 2 loops — called trh or treble half —, miss 1tr, work trh into next tr, yrh and draw through all 3 loops on hook, 1ch, *work trh into same st as before, miss 1tr, work trh into next tr, yrh and draw through all 3 loops on hook, 1ch, rep from * to end, 1tr into 3rd of first 3ch.
3rd row 3ch to count as first tr, 1ch, work trh into next 1ch sp, trh into next 1ch sp, yrh and draw through all 3 loops on hook, 1ch, *work trh into same 1ch sp as before, trh into next 1ch sp, yrh and draw through all 3 loops on hook, 1ch, rep from * to end, 1tr into 3rd of first 3ch.
The 3rd row forms the pattern.

Checked and diagonal pattern
Make a number of chain divisible by 3 plus 2 and 2 extra turning chain.
1st row (WS) Into 4th ch from hook work 1tr, 1tr into each ch to end.
2nd row 3ch to count as first tr, *1tr into each of next 3tr, yrh twice, insert hook from right to left round the stem of the tr below the first of these 3tr and complete as for dtr, rep from * to end, 1tr into 3rd of first 3ch.
3rd row 4ch to count as first dtr, *miss 1dtr, 1dtr into each of next 3tr, rep from * to end, 1dtr into 3rd of first 3ch.
4th row 3ch, *miss next 2dtr, work 1dtr round stem of next dtr then keeping hook behind this dtr work 1tr into each of the 2 missed dtr and 1tr into top of same dtr as the one worked round, rep from * to end, 1tr into 4th of first 4ch.
5th row 4ch to count as first dtr, *1dtr into each of next 3tr, miss next dtr, rep from * to end, 1dtr into 3rd of first 3ch.
6th row 3ch to count as first tr, *1tr into each of next 3dtr, 1dtr round stem of the first of these 3dtr, rep from * to end, 1tr into 4th of first 4ch.
The 3rd to 6th rows form the pattern.

Raised flower pattern
Make a number of chain divisible by 6 plus 1 and 1 extra turning chain.
1st row (RS) Into 3rd ch from hook work 1htr, 1htr into each ch to end.
2nd row 2ch to count as first htr, 1htr between each htr to end.
Rep 2nd row twice more.
5th row 2ch to count as first htr, work (1htr between htr) 3 times, *work 6tr round the stem of the next htr on 4th row, turn and work 6tr round stem of preceding htr on 4th row, join with a ss to first tr, turn again and cont along row, work (1htr between htr) 6 times, rep from * to end, ending with (1htr between htr) 3 times.
6th to 10th rows As 2nd.
11th row 2ch to count as first htr, work (1htr between htr) 6 times, *work 6tr round the stem of the next htr on 10th row, turn and work 6tr round stem of preceding htr on 10th row, join with a ss to first tr, turn again and cont along row, work (1htr between htr) 6 times, rep from * to end.
12th and 13th rows As 2nd.
The 2nd to 13th rows form the pattern.

Brick pattern

Brick pattern in panels

Crazy pattern

Florette pattern

Close fabric stitch

Forget-me-not stitch

Spaced treble groups

Checked and diagonal pattern

Raised flower pattern

Coloured patterns

Raised trebles in two colours
Using A, make a number of chain divisible by 2 plus 1 and 2 extra turning chain.
1st row (RS) Into 4th ch from hook work 1tr, 1tr into each ch to end.
2nd row 1ch to count as first dc, 1dc into each tr to end working last dc into 3rd of first 3ch.

and joining in B as given in Chapter 9.
3rd row Using B, 1ch to count as first dc, *work 1RtF round stem of next tr on first row as given in Chapter 20, miss 1dc of 2nd row, 1dc into next dc, rep from * to end working last dc into first ch.
4th row Using B, 1ch to count as first dc, 1dc into each st to end working last dc into first ch

and joining in A.
5th row Using A, as 3rd, working RtF round stem of RtF.
6th row Using A, as 4th.
The 3rd to 6th rows form the pattern.

Chevron pattern in two colours
Using A, make a number of chain divisible by 13 plus 1 and 2 extra turning chain.
1st row (RS) Into 3rd ch from hook work 1dc, *1dc into each of next 5ch, miss 2ch, 1dc into each of next 5ch, 3dc into next ch, rep from * to end working only 2dc into last ch.

2nd row 1ch to count as first dc, 1dc into first dc (edge st), *1dc into each of next 5dc, miss 2dc, 1dc into each of next 5dc, 3dc into next dc, rep from * to end, ending with 2dc into turning ch and changing colour on last st as given in Chapter 9.
3rd row Using B, as 2nd row but do

not change colour.
4th row Using B, as 2nd row.
5th row Using A, as 3rd row.
6th row Using A, as 2nd row.
The 3rd to 6th rows form the pattern.

Shell pattern in two colours
Using A, make a number of chain divisible by 6 plus 1 and 3 extra turning chain.
1st row (RS) Into 4th ch from hook work 2tr, *miss 2ch, 1dc into next ch, miss 2ch, 5tr into next ch, rep from * to end, ending with 3tr into last ch and changing colour on last st as given in Chapter 9. *Turn.*

2nd row Using B, 1ch to count as first dc, *5tr into next dc, 1dc into 3rd of 5tr, rep from * to end working last dc into 3rd of first 3ch. *Do not turn.* Leave loop of B for time being.
3rd row Return to beg of 2nd row, using A pull yarn through first ch on to hook, 3ch to count as first tr, 2tr into first 1ch, *1dc into 3rd of 5tr, 5tr into next dc, rep from * to end, ending

with 3tr into last dc and changing colour on last st. Turn.
The 2nd and 3rd rows form the pattern.

Fish-scale pattern in two colours
Using A, make a number of chain divisible by 6 plus 1 and 3 extra turning chain.
1st row (RS) Into 4th ch from hook work 2tr, *miss 2ch, 1dc into next ch, miss 2ch, 5tr into next ch, rep from * to end, ending with 3tr into last ch and changing colour on last st as given in Chapter 9. *Turn.*
2nd row Using B, 1ch to count as first dc, *2ch,

yrh, insert hook into next tr and draw a loop through, yrh and draw through 2 loops on hook — called trh —, work trh into next tr, into next dc then into each of next 2tr, (6 loops on hook), yrh and draw through all 6 loops on hook, 2ch, 1dc into next tr, rep from * to end working last dc into 3rd of first 3ch. *Do not turn.* Leave loop of B for time being.
3rd row Return to beg of 2nd row, using A pull

yarn through first ch on to hook, 3ch to count as first tr, 2tr into first 1ch (edge st), *1dc into top of group, 5tr into next dc, rep from * to end, ending with 3tr into last dc and changing colour on last st. *Turn.*
The 2nd and 3rd rows form the pattern.

Three-clour check pattern
Using A, make a number of chain divisible by 4 plus 2 and 2 extra turning chain.
1st row (RS) Into 4th ch from hook work 1tr, *2ch, miss 2ch, 1tr into each of next 2ch, rep from * to end, joining in B on last st as given in Chapter 9.
2nd row Using B, *2ch, miss first 2tr, 1tr into each of the 2 missed ch of commencing ch, rep from * to end, ending with 2ch, miss next tr, ss

into 3rd of first 3ch joining in C.
3rd row Using C, 3ch to count as first tr, 1tr into next tr of first row, *2ch, miss 2tr of 2nd row, 1tr into each of next 2tr of 1st row, rep from * to end joining in A on last st.
4th row Using A, *2ch, miss first 2tr, 1tr into each of next 2tr on 2nd row, rep from * to end, ending with 2ch, miss 1tr, ss into 3rd of first 3ch joining in B.
The 3rd and 4th rows form the pattern, working

1 row in each colour throughout. To avoid a row of holes in the final casting off row, use the next colour and either a 3rd or 4th row but instead of working '2ch, miss 2tr', work 1dc into each of these 2tr then 1tr into each of the next 2tr on previous row.

Three-colour broken stripe pattern
Using A, make a number of chain divisible by 2 plus 1 and 2 extra turning chain.
1st row (RS) Into 3rd ch from hook work 1htr, * miss 1ch, 2htr into next ch, rep from * to end joining in B on last st as given in Chapter 9.

2nd row Using B, 2ch to count as first htr, *work 2htr between next 2 pairs of htr, rep from * to end, ending with 2htr between last 2 pair, 1htr into 2nd of first 2ch, joining in C.
3rd row Using C, 2ch to count as first htr, 1htr between first htr and next pair, *2htr between

next 2 pairs of htr, rep from * to end working last 2htr between last pair and first 2ch, joining in A.
The 2nd and 3rd rows form the pattern, working 1 row in each colour throughout.

Two-colour openwork pattern
Using A, make a number of chain divisible by 5 plus 3 and 2 extra turning chain.
1st row (RS) Into 6th ch from hook work 2tr, 2ch, 2tr into next ch, *miss 3ch, 2tr into next ch, 2ch, 2tr into next ch, rep from * to last 3ch, miss 2ch, 1tr into last ch.

2nd row 3ch to count as first tr, *work (2tr, 2ch, 2tr) into 2ch sp, rep from * to end working 1tr into 3rd of first 5ch, joining in B on last st as given in Chapter 9.
3rd row Using B, as 2nd row but working last tr into 3rd of first 3ch and do not change colour.
4th row Using B, as 3rd row, joining in A.

The 3rd row forms the pattern, working 2 rows in each colour throughout and using more colours if required, always making sure that you leave the yarn at the end you want for next time, to avoid breaking off the yarn.

Two-colour broken stripe pattern
Using A, make a number of chain divisible by 4 plus 1 and 1 extra turning chain.
1st row (RS) Into 3rd ch from hook work 1dc, 1dc into each ch to end.
2nd row 1ch to count as first dc, 1dc into each dc to end working last dc into 2nd of first 2ch

and joining in B on last st as given in Chapter 9.
3rd row Using B, 1ch to count as first dc, 1dc into next dc, *1dc into next dc inserting hook 1 row below, 1dc into each of next 3dc, rep from * to last 3dc, 1dc into next dc inserting hook 1 row below, 1dc into next dc, 1dc into first ch.
4th row Using B, as 2nd row working last dc

into first ch and joining in A.
5th row Using A, 1ch to count as first dc, *1dc into each of next 3dc, 1dc into next dc inserting hook 1 row below, rep from * to last 4dc, 1dc into each of next 3dc, 1dc into first ch.
The 2nd to 5th rows form the pattern.

Three-colour speckle pattern
Using A, make a number of chain divisible by 2 plus 1 and 2 extra turning chain.
1st row (RS) Into 3rd ch from hook work 1tr, *miss 1ch, work 1dc and 1tr into next ch, rep

from * to last 2ch, miss 1ch, 1dc into last ch joining in B as given in Chapter 9.
2nd row Using B, 1ch to count as first dc, 1tr into edge st, *work 1dc and 1tr into next dc, rep from * to end, ending with 1dc into 2nd of first

2ch, joining in C.
3rd row Using C, as 2nd row working last dc into first ch and joining in A.
The 2nd row forms the pattern, working one row in each colour throughout.

Raised trebles in two colours

Chevron pattern in two colours

Shell pattern in two colours

Fish-scale pattern in two colours

Three-colour check pattern

Three-colour broken stripe pattern

Two-colour openwork pattern

Two-colour broken stripe pattern

Three-colour speckle pattern

More large patterns

Window panes
Make a number of chain divisible by 18 plus 10 and 2 extra turning chain.

1st row (RS) Into 4th ch from hook work 1tr, 1tr into each of next 8ch, *8ch, miss 8ch, 1tr into each of next 10ch, rep from * to end.

2nd row 3ch to count as first tr, 1tr into next tr, (2ch, miss 2tr, 1tr into each of next 2tr) twice, *8ch, (1tr into each of next 2tr, 2ch, miss 2tr) twice, 1tr into each of next 2tr, rep from * to end working last tr into 3rd of first 3ch.

3rd row 3ch to count as first tr, 1tr into next tr, (2tr into 2ch sp, 1tr into each of next 2tr) twice, *8ch, (1tr into each of next 2tr, 2tr into 2ch sp) twice, 1tr into each of next 2tr, rep from * to end working last tr into 3rd of first 3ch.

4th row 3ch to count as first tr, 1tr into next tr, (2ch, miss 2tr, 1tr into each of next 2tr) twice, *4ch, insert hook under 3 strands of 8ch and work 1dc linking the 3 strands tog, 4ch, (1tr into each of next 2tr, 2ch, miss 2tr) twice, 1tr into each of next 2tr, rep from * to end working last tr into 3rd of first 3ch.

5th row As 3rd.

6th row 3ch to count as first tr, 8ch, miss 8tr, 1tr into next tr, *1tr into each of next 8ch, 1tr into next tr, 8ch, miss 8tr, 1tr into next tr, rep from * to end working last tr into 3rd of first 3ch.

7th row 3ch to count as first tr, 8ch, *(1tr into each of next 2tr, 2ch, miss 2tr) twice, 1tr into each of next 2tr, 8ch, rep from * to last st, 1tr into 3rd of first 3ch.

8th row 3ch to count as first tr, 8ch, *(1tr into each of next 2tr, 2tr into 2ch sp) twice, 1tr into each of next 2tr, 8ch, rep from * to last st, 1tr into 3rd of first 3ch.

9th row 3ch to count as first tr, 4ch, insert hook under 3 strands of 8ch and work 1dc linking the 3 strands tog, 4ch, *(1tr into each of next 2tr, 2ch, miss 2tr) twice, 1tr into each of next 2tr, 4ch, 1dc linking 3 strands of 8ch tog, 4ch, rep from * to last st, 1tr into 3rd of first 3ch.

10th row As 8th.

11th row 3ch to count as first tr, 1tr into each of next 8ch, 1tr into next tr, *8ch, miss 8tr, 1tr into next tr, 1tr into each of next 8ch, 1tr into next tr, rep from * to end working last tr into 3rd of first 3ch.

The 2nd to 11th rows form the pattern.

Japanese fans
Make a number of chain divisible by 14 plus 1 and 1 extra turning chain.

1st row (WS) Into 3rd ch from hook work 1dc, 1dc into each ch to end.

2nd row 1ch to count as first dc, *miss 6dc, yrh, insert hook into next dc and draw loop through pulling the loop up to a height of 1.5cm ($\frac{1}{2}$in), yrh and draw through 2 loops, yrh and draw through rem 2 loops — called 1 long tr —, work 12 more long tr into same dc, miss 6dc, 1dc into next dc, rep from * to end working last dc into 2nd of first 2ch.

3rd row 4ch to count as first long tr, 1 long tr into first dc (edge st), *5ch, 1dc into 7th of 13 long tr, 5ch, 2 long tr into next dc, rep from * to end working last 2 long tr into first ch.

4th row 1ch to count as first dc, *13 long tr into next dc, 1dc between next 2 long tr, rep from * to end working last dc between last long tr and first 4ch.

The 3rd and 4th rows form the pattern.

Flower pattern
Make a number of chain divisible by 20 plus 1 and 5 extra turning chain.

1st row (RS) Into 10th ch from hook work 1tr, * 3ch, (yrh twice, insert hook into top of last tr worked and draw loop through, (yrh and draw through 2 loops) twice, (2 loops rem on hook) — called half dtr —, work another half dtr into same place, yrh and draw through all 3 loops on hook — called 1ClA or 1 Cluster A —, miss 3ch, work 3 half dtr into next ch, yrh and draw through all 4 loops on hook — called 1C1B or 1 Cluster B —, miss 3ch, 1ClB into next ch, 1ClA into top of Cl just worked, miss 3ch, 1tr into next ch, 5ch, miss 3ch, 1dc into next ch, 5ch, miss 3ch, 1tr into next ch, rep from * to end, omitting last 5ch and 1tr.

2nd row 1ch to count as first dc, *5ch, 1tr into tr, 3ch, work (1ClB, 3ch and 1ClB) into top of 2ClB of previous row, 3ch, 1tr into next tr, 5ch, 1dc into next dc, rep from * to end working last dc into 4th of first 9ch.

3rd row 3ch to count as first, tr, *miss 1ch, 1ClB into next ch, 1ClA into top of Cl just worked, 1tr into next tr, 5ch, 1dc into 3ch sp between 2Cl, 1tr into next tr, 1ClA into top of tr just worked, miss 3ch, 1ClB into next ch, miss 1ch and 1dc, rep from * to end but after last ClB work 1tr into first ch.

4th row 3ch to count as first tr, 1ch, 1ClB into top of first 1ClB, *3ch, 1tr into next tr, 5ch, 1dc into next dc, 5ch, 1tr into next tr, 3ch, (1ClB, 3ch, 1ClB) into top of 2 ClB of previous row, rep from * to end, ending with 1ClB into top of last 1ClB, 1ch, 1tr into 3rd of first 3ch.

5th row 1ch to count as first dc, *5ch, 1tr into next tr, 1ClA into top of tr just worked, miss 3ch, 1ClB into next ch, miss 1ch, 1dc and 1ch, work 1ClB into next ch, 1ClA into top of Cl just workrd, 1tr into next tr, 5ch, 1dc into 3ch sp between 2 Cl, rep from * to end working last dc into 3rd of first 3ch.

The 2nd to 5th rows form the pattern, ending 2nd row by working last dc into first ch.

Diagonal raised pattern
Make a number of chain divisible by 8 plus 6 and 2 extra turning chain.

1st row (WS) Into 4th ch from hook work 1tr, 1tr into each ch to end.

Note: Before working next row refer to Basket stitch in Chapter 20, for working method of RtF and RtB.

2nd row 3ch to count as first tr, 1RtF round each of next 4tr, *1RtB round each of next 4tr, 1RtF round each of next 4tr, rep from * to end, 1tr into 3rd of first 3ch.

3rd row 3ch to count as first tr, work 4RtB, * 4RtF, 4RtB, rep from * to last st, 1tr into 3rd of first 3ch.

4th row 3ch to count as first tr, work 3RtF, *4RtB, 4RtF, rep from * to last 2 sts, 1RtB, 1tr into 3rd of first 3ch.

5th row 3ch to count as first tr, work 1RtF, *4RtB, 4RtF, rep from * to last 4 sts, 3RtB, 1tr into 3rd of first 3ch.

6th row 3ch to count as first tr, work 2RtF, *4RtB, 4RtF, rep from * to last 3 sts, 2RtB, 1tr into 3rd of of first 3ch.

7th row As 6th.

8th row As 5th.

9th row As 4th.

10th row As 3rd.

11th row As 2nd.

12th row 3ch to count as first tr, work 3RtB, *4RtF, 4RtB, rep from * to last 2 sts, 1RtF, 1tr into 3rd of first 3ch.

13th row 3ch to count as first tr, work 1RtB, *4RtF, 4RtB, rep from * to last 4 sts, 3RtF, 1tr into 3rd of first 3ch.

14th row 3ch to count as first tr, work 2RtB, *4RtF, 4RtB, rep from * to last 3 sts, 2RtF, 1tr into 3rd of first 3ch.

15th row As 14th.

16th row As 13th.

17th row As 12th.

The 2nd to 17th rows form the pattern.

Openwork chevron pattern
Make a number of chain divisible by 14 and 2 extra turning chain.

1st row (RS) Into 4th ch from hook work 1tr, 1tr into each of next 5ch, *2ch, 1tr into each of next 14ch, rep from * to last 7ch, 2ch, 1tr into each of next 7ch.

2nd row Miss first tr (edge st), ss into next tr, 3ch to count as first tr, 1ch, miss 1tr, (1tr into next tr, 1ch, miss 1tr) twice, *(1tr, 3ch, 1tr) into 2ch sp, (1ch, miss 1tr, 1tr into next tr) 3 times, (1ch, miss 1tr, 1tr into next tr) 3 times, rep from * to last 2ch sp, (1tr, 3ch, 1tr) into 2ch sp, (1ch, miss 1tr, 1tr into next tr) 3 times but do not work into turning chain, turn.

3rd row Miss first tr (edge st), ss into 1ch sp, 3ch to count as first tr, * (1tr into next tr, 1tr into 1ch sp) twice, (2tr, 2ch, 2tr) into 3ch sp, miss next tr, (1tr into 1ch sp, 1tr into next tr) twice, 1tr into next 1ch sp, miss 2tr, (1tr into next 1ch sp, 1tr into next tr) twice, 1tr into next 1ch sp, rep from * to last 3ch sp, (2tr, 2ch, 2tr) into 3ch sp, miss next tr, (1tr into 1ch sp, 1tr into next tr) twice, 1tr into next 1ch sp but do not work into turning ch, turn.

The 2nd and 3rd rows form the pattern.

Star pattern in panels
Make a number of chain divisible by 22 plus 1 and 2 extra turning chain.

1st row (RS) Into 4th ch from hook work 1tr, 1tr into each of next 2ch, *(5ch, miss 2ch, 1dc into each of next 3ch, 5ch, miss 2ch, 1tr into next ch) twice, 1tr into each of next 6ch, rep from * to end, ending with 1tr into each of last 3ch.

2nd row 1ch to count as first dc, 1dc into each of next 3tr, *(1dc into first ch of 5ch loop, 4ch, 1tr into 2nd of 3dc, 4ch, 1dc into last ch of 5ch loop, 1dc into next tr) twice, 1dc into each of next 6tr, rep from * to end, ending with 1dc into each of last 2tr, 1dc into 3rd of first 3ch.

3rd row 1ch to count as first dc, 1dc into each of next 4dc, *(5ch, 1tr into next tr, 5ch, 1dc into each of next 3dc) twice, 1dc into each of next 5dc, rep from * to end, ending with 1dc into last

Window panes

Japanese fans

Flower pattern

Diagonal raised pattern

Openwork chevron pattern

Star pattern in panels

49

dc, 1dc into first ch.

4th row 3ch to count as first tr, 1tr into each of next 3dc, *(4ch, 1dc into last ch of 5ch loop, 1dc into next tr, 1dc into first ch of next 5ch loop, 4ch, 1tr into 2nd of 3dc) twice, 1tr into each of next 6dc, rep from * to end, ending with

5th row 3ch to count as first tr, 1tr into each of next 3tr, *(5ch, 1dc into each of next 3dc, 5ch, 1tr into next tr) twice, 1tr into each of next 6tr, rep from * to end, ending with 1tr into each of last 2dc, 1tr into first ch.

5th row 3ch to count as first tr, 1tr into each of next 3tr, *(5ch, 1dc into each of next 3dc, 5ch, 1tr into next tr) twice, 1tr into each of next 6tr, rep from * to end, ending with 1tr into each of last 2tr, 1tr into 3rd of first 3ch.

The 2nd and 5th rows form the pattern. The panels could be varied in width by rep the figures in brackets more times, noting that 6 extra ch are required for each extra rep, or fewer or more tr could be worked between each panel.

Spiral motifs

Spiral motif

Make 6ch. Join with a ss to first ch to form circle.

1st round 1ch, work 12dc into circle. Do not join this or subsequent rounds.

2nd round Work 2dc into each dc to end. 24dc.

3rd round *1dc into each of next 3dc, 3ch, miss 1dc, rep from * 5 times more.

4th round *1dc into each of next 3dc, 2dc into 3ch sp, 3ch, rep from * 5 times more.

5th round *Miss 1dc, 1dc into each of next 4dc, 2dc into 3ch sp, 4ch, rep from * 5 times more.

6th round *Miss 1dc, 1dc into each of next 5dc, 2dc into 4ch sp, 4ch, rep from * 5 times more.

7th round *Miss 1dc, 1dc into each of rem dc of group, 2dc into ch loop, 5ch, rep from * 5 times more.

Rep 7th round 5 times more.

13th round Miss 1dc, ss into next dc, 2ch to count as next dc, 1dc into each of next 10dc, 5tr

into next dc, 2dc into ch loop, *miss 1dc, 1dc into each of next 11dc, 5tr into next dc, 2dc into ch loop, rep from * 4 times more. Join with a ss to 2nd of first 2ch. Fasten off.

This motif can be increased in size by working the 7th round as many times as necessary, noting that when working the edging there will be one more dc in each group for every extra repeat of the 7th round.

Six-sided motif

Make 10ch. Join with a ss to first ch to form circle.

1st round 3ch to count as first tr, work 23tr into circle. Join with a ss to 3rd of first 3ch. 24tr.

2nd round 3ch to count as first tr, 3tr into ss at base of 3ch, *miss 1tr, 1dc into next tr, miss 1tr, 7tr into next tr, rep from * 4 times more, miss 1tr, 1dc into next tr, miss 1tr, 3tr into ss at end of 1st round. Join with a ss to 3rd of first 3ch.

3rd round 3ch, 1dc into ss at base of 3ch, *7ch, work (1dc, 3ch, 1dc) into 4th of next 7tr, rep from * 4 times more, 7ch, ss into 3ch loop at beg of round.

4th round 3ch, 3tr into first 3ch loop, *5ch, 1dc into 7ch loop, 5ch, 7tr into 3ch loop, rep from * 4 times more, 5ch, 1dc into 7ch loop, 5ch, 3tr into 3ch loop at beg of round. Join with a ss to 3rd of first 3ch.

5th round 3ch, 3tr into ss at base of 3ch, *(5ch, 1dc into next 5ch loop) twice, 5ch, 7tr into 4th

of 7tr, rep from * 4 times more, (5ch, 1dc into next 5ch loop) twice, 5ch, 3tr into ss at end of round. Join with a ss to 3rd of first 3ch.

6th round As 5th, working the instructions in brackets 3 times instead of twice.

7th round As 5th, working the instructions in brackets 4 times. Fasten off.

To increase the size of the motif, continue repeating the 5th round, working the instructions in brackets once more for each round.

Rose square

This motif is worked in 4 colours. Using A, make 6ch. Join with a ss to first ch to form circle.

1st round 3ch to count as first tr, *2ch, 1tr into circle, rep from * 6 times more, 2ch. Join with a ss to 3rd of first 3ch.

2nd round Into each 2ch sp work (1dc, 1htr, 3tr, 1htr, 1dc). Join with a ss to ss at end of 1st round.

3rd round *4ch, 1dc into back of next tr of 1st round, rep from * 6 times more, 4ch. Join with a ss to ss at end of 2nd round, keeping each 4ch loop behind the petals of the 2nd round.

4th round Into each 4ch loop work (1dc, 1htr, 5tr, 1htr, 1dc). Join with a ss to ss at end of 3rd round.

5th round As 3rd working into the back of the dc of 3rd round. Break off A.

6th round Join in B to ss at end of last round, into each 4ch loop work (1dc, 1htr, 7tr, 1htr, 1dc). Join with a ss to ss at end of 5th round.

7th round Using B, as 3rd working into the back of the dc of 5th round.

8th round Using B, into each 4ch loop work (1dc, 1htr, 2tr, 5dtr, 2tr, 1htr, 1dc). Join with a ss to ss at end of 7th round. Break off B.

9th round Join C to centre dtr of any petal, 1ch to count as first dc, 7ch, keeping last loop of each dtr on hook work 3dtr into centre dtr of next petal, yrh and draw through all 4 loops on hook — called 1Cl or cluster —, (4ch, 1Cl) twice into same dtr, *7ch, 1dc into centre dtr of next petal, 7ch, (1Cl, 4ch, 1Cl, 4ch, 1Cl) into centre dtr of next petal, rep from * twice more, 7ch. Join with a ss to first ch. Break off C.

10th round Join D to centre 1Cl of one corner,

3ch to count as first tr, 3ch, 3tr into top of same 1Cl, *1ch, 3tr into next 4ch loop, 1ch, (3tr, 1ch, 3tr) into next 7ch loop, 1ch, (3tr, 1ch, 3tr) into next 7ch loop, 1ch, 3tr into next 4ch loop, 1ch, **, (3tr, 3ch, 3tr) into centre 1Cl at corner, *, rep from * to * twice more then from * to ** once more, 2tr into top of 1Cl at first corner. Join with a ss to 3rd of first 3ch.

11th round Using D, ss into first 3ch sp, 3ch to count as first tr, 3ch, 3tr into 3ch sp, *(1ch, 3tr into next 1ch sp) 7 times, 1ch, **, (3tr, 3ch, 3tr) into 3ch sp at corner, *, rep from * to * twice more, then from * to ** once more, 2tr into last 3ch sp. Join with a ss to 3rd of first 3ch.

12th round Using D, as 11th, working (1ch, 3tr into next 1ch sp) 8 times instead of 7. Fasten off.

Square motif with bobbles

Make 6ch. Join with a ss to first ch to form circle.

1st round 1ch to count as first dc, work 11dc into circle. Join with a ss to first ch. 12dc.

2nd round 3ch to count as first tr, 1tr into same place, (yrh, insert hook into next dc and draw a loop through, yrh and draw through 2 loops on hook) 6 times into same dc, yrh and draw through 6 loops on hook, yrh and draw through rem 2 loops on hook — called Bl or bobble —, *2tr into each of next 2dc, Bl into next dc, rep from * twice more, 2tr into next dc. Join with a ss to 3rd of first 3ch.

3rd round 3ch to count as first tr, 1tr into same place, *1tr into each of next 3 sts, 2tr into next st, 1ch, 2tr into next st, rep from * twice more, 1tr into each of next 3 sts, 2tr into next st, 1ch. Join with a ss to 3rd of first 3ch.

4th round 3ch to count as first tr, 1tr into same place, *(1tr into next tr, Bl into next tr) twice, 1tr into next tr, 2tr into next tr, 2ch, 2tr into next tr, rep from * 3 times more omitting last 2tr. Join with a ss to 3rd of first 3ch.

5th round 3ch to count as first tr, 1tr into same place, *1tr into each of next 7 sts, 2tr into next st, 3ch, 2tr into next st, rep from * 3 times more omitting last 2tr. Join with a ss to 3rd of first 3ch.

6th round 3ch to count as first tr, 1tr into same place, *1tr into each of next 2tr, (Bl into next tr, 1tr into next tr) 3 times, 1tr into next tr, 2tr into next tr, 4ch, 2tr into next tr, rep from * 3 times more omitting last 2tr. Join with a ss to 3rd of first 3ch.

7th round 3ch to count as first tr, 1tr into same place, *1tr into each of next 11 sts, 2tr into next st, 5ch, 2tr into next st, rep from * 3 times more omitting last 2tr. Join with a ss to 3rd of first 3ch. Fasten off.

Danish square

This motif is worked in 3 colours. Using A, make 10ch. Join with a ss to first ch to form circle.

1st round 1ch to count as first dc, work 19dc into circle. Join with a ss to first ch. 20dc.

2nd round 1ch to count as first dc, *7ch, miss 4dc, 1dc into next dc, rep from * 3 times more omitting last dc. Join with a ss to first ch.

3rd round 1ch to count as first dc, *9dc into

7ch loop, 1dc into next dc, rep from * 3 times more omitting last dc. Join with a ss to first ch. Break off A.

4th round Join B to 5th of 9dc at any corner, 1ch to count as first dc, 2dc into same dc, *1dc into each of next 9dc, 3dc into next dc, rep from * 3 times more omitting last 3dc. Join with a ss to first ch. Break off B.

5th round Join C to 2nd of 3dc at any corner, 3ch to count as first tr, 2ch, 1tr into same dc, *(1ch, miss 1dc, 1tr into next dc) 5 times, 1ch, miss 1dc, (1tr, 2ch, 1tr) into next dc, rep from * twice more, (1ch, miss 1dc, 1tr into next dc) 5 times, 1ch. Join with a ss to 3rd of first 3ch. Break off C.

6th round Join A to 2ch sp at any corner, 1ch to count as first dc, 2dc into same sp, *(1dc into next tr, 1dc into 1ch sp) 6 times, 1dc into next tr, 3dc into 2ch sp, rep from * 3 times more omitting last 3dc. Join with a ss to first ch.

7th round Using A, ss into next dc, 3ch to count as first tr, 2ch, 1tr into same dc, *(1ch, miss 1dc, 1tr into next dc) 7 times, 1ch, miss 1dc, (1tr, 2ch, 1tr) into next dc, rep from * twice more, (1ch, miss 1dc, 1tr into next dc) 7 times, 1ch. Join with

a ss to 3rd of first 3ch. Break off A.

8th round Join B to 2ch sp at any corner, work as 6th round, repeating the instructions in brackets 8 times instead of 6.

9th round Using B, as 7th, working the instructions in brackets 9 times. Break off B.

10th round Join C to 2ch sp at any corner, work

as 6th round, repeating instructions in brackets 10 times.

11th round Using C, as 7th round, working instructions in brackets 11 times. Break off C.

12th round Using A, as 6th round, working instructions in brackets 12 times. Fasten off.

Norwegian motif

Make 4ch. Join with a ss to first ch to form circle.

1st round 1ch to count as first dc, work 7dc into circle. Join with a ss to first ch, 8dc.

2nd round 4ch to count as first dtr, *2ch, 1dtr into next dc, 5ch, 1dtr into next dc, rep from * 3 times more omitting last dtr. Join with a ss to 4th of first 4ch.

3rd round 1ch to count as first dc, *2dc into 2ch sp, 1dc into next dtr, (3dc, 2ch, 3dc) into 5ch loop, 1dc into next dtr, rep from * 3 times more omitting last dc. Join with a ss to first ch.

4th round 4ch,(yrh twice, insert hook into next

dc and draw loop through, yrh and draw through 2 loops, yrh and draw through 2 loops — called dtrh —) into each of next 3dc, yrh and draw through all 4 loops on hook, *7ch, 1dc into next 2ch sp, 7ch, miss 3dc, work dtrh into each of next 4dc, yrh and draw through all loops on hook, rep from * twice more, 7ch, 1dc into 2ch sp, 7ch. Join with a ss to top of first cluster.

5th round 1ch to count as first dc, 2dc into top of same cluster, *1dc into each of next 7ch, 1dc into next dc, 1dc into each of next 7ch, 3dc into top of next cluster, rep from * 3 times more omitting last 3dc. Join with a ss to first ch.

6th round Ss into each of next 2dc, *1dc into

next dc, 5ch, miss 4dc, 1dc into next dc, 5ch, miss 3dc, 1dc into next dc, 5ch, miss 4dc, 1dc into next dc, 7ch, miss 3dc, rep from * 3 times more. Join with a ss to first dc.

7th round Ss into first 5ch loop, 3ch to count as first tr, (2tr, 3ch, 3tr) into same loop, (3tr, 3ch, 3tr) into each of next two 5ch loops, *(3tr, 3ch, 3tr, 3ch, 3tr) into 7ch loop, (3tr, 3ch, 3tr) into each of next three 5ch loops, rep from * twice more, (3tr, 3ch, 3tr, 3ch, 3tr) into 7ch loop. Join with a ss to 3rd of first 3ch. Fasten off.

Spiders web motif

Make 8ch. Join with a ss to first ch to form circle.

1st round 3ch to count as first tr, work 23tr into circle. Join with a ss to 3rd of first 3ch. 24tr.

2nd round 3ch to count as first tr, 1tr into each of next 2tr, 3ch, *1tr into each of next 3tr, 3ch, rep from * 6 times more. Join with a ss to 3rd of first 3ch.

3rd round 3ch to count as first tr, 1tr into each of next 2tr, 8ch, *1tr into each of next 3tr, 8ch, rep from * 6 times more. Join with a ss to 3rd of first 3ch.

4th round 3ch to count as first tr, 1tr into each of next 2tr, *4ch, 1dc into 8ch loop, 4ch, 1tr into each of next 3tr, rep from * 7 times more omitting last 3tr. Join with ss to 3rd of first 3ch.

5th round 3ch to count as first tr, 1tr into each of next 2tr, *4ch, 1dc into 4ch loop, 1dc into next dc, 1dc into 4ch loop, 4ch, 1tr into each of next 3tr, rep from * 7 times more omitting last 3tr. Join with a ss to 3rd of first 3ch.

6th round 3ch to count as first tr, 1tr into each of next 2tr, *4ch, 1dc into 4ch loop, 1dc into each of next 3dc, 1dc into 4ch loop, 4ch, 1tr into each of next 3tr, rep from * 7 times more omitting last 3tr. Join with a ss to 3rd of first 3ch.

7th round 3ch to count as first tr, 1tr into each of next 2tr, *5ch, miss 1dc, 1dc into each of next 3dc, miss 1dc, 5ch, 1tr into each of next 3tr, rep from * 7 times more omitting last 3tr. Join with a ss to 3rd of first 3ch.

8th round 3ch to count as first tr, 1tr into each of next 2tr, *4ch, miss 1dc, (1dtr, 4ch, 1dtr) into next dc, miss 1dc, 4ch, 1tr into each of next 3tr, rep from * 7 times more omitting last 3tr. Join with a ss to 3rd of first 3ch.

9th round 1ch to count as first dc, 1dc into each of next 2tr, *5dc into each of next three 4ch loops, 1dc into each of next 3tr, rep from * 7 times more omitting last 3dc. Join with a ss to first ch. Fasten off.

Star of Eve motif

Make 4ch. Join with a ss to first ch to form circle.

1st round 3ch to count as first tr, work 11tr into circle. Join with a ss to 3rd of first 3ch.

2nd round *6ch, ss into 3rd ch from hook, 4ch, ss into next tr, rep from * to end working last ss into ss at end of 1st round. Fasten off.

Small round motif

This motif is useful as a filler between larger motifs. Make 12ch. Join with a ss to first ch to form circle.

1st round 3ch, (yrh, insert hook into circle and draw a loop through, yrh and draw through 2 loops on hook — called trh —) twice, yrh and

draw through all 3 loops on hook, *3ch, work trh 3 times into circle, yrh and draw through all 4 loops on hook — called 1Cl —, rep from * 6 times more, 3ch. Join with a ss to top of first 1Cl.

2nd round 3ch to count as first tr, 2ch, 1tr into top of same 1Cl, *(1tr, 2ch, 1tr) into 3ch sp, (1tr, 2ch, 1tr) into top of next 1Cl, rep from * 6 times more, (1tr, 2ch, 1tr) into 3ch sp. Join with a ss to 3rd of first 3ch. Fasten off.

Top row, left : Spiral motif
Top row, centre : Spider's web motif
Top row, right : Six-sided motif
Centre : Danish square
Centre left : Norwegian motif
Centre right : Square motif with bobbles
Bottom left : Star of Eve motif
Bottom centre : Rose motif
Bottom right : Small round motif

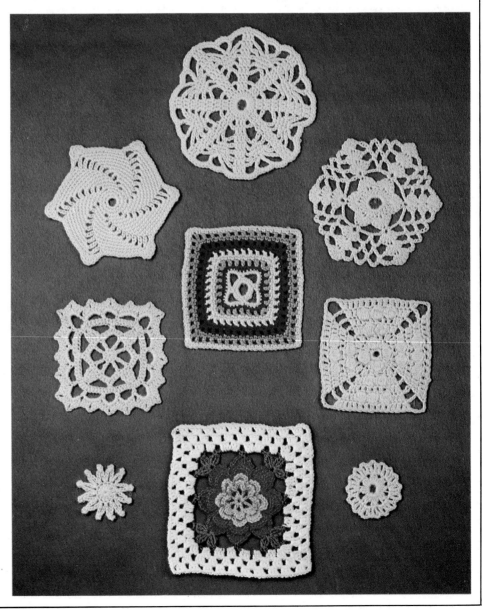

51

Filet crochet patterns

Filet crochet is normally worked from a chart and before beginning any of these patterns, you should study the following explanations of the working methods for each symbol shown on these charts.

Block

A block is shown as a cross on the charts and consists of 3tr. When 1 block stands alone there will be 4tr in the group, the first of which belongs to the previous space. When 2 blocks stand alone there will be 7tr in the group, 3 for each block and 1 for the previous space. Therefore, all groups of blocks will have 3 times as many trebles as there are crosses, plus 1 treble. When working the block into a space, work the first 2tr into the space and the 3rd tr into the next tr.

Space

A space is shown as an open square on the charts and consists of 2ch, miss 2ch or 2tr, 1tr into next tr for each space.

Lacet

A lacet is shown as a 'V' on the charts, taking up 2 squares, and consists of 3ch, miss 2ch or 2tr, 1dc into next st, 3ch, miss 2ch or 2tr, 1tr into next st.

Bar

A bar is shown as a line taking up 2 squares in width on the charts and consists of 5ch, miss 1 lacet or 5 sts, 1tr into next st.

Note On all the charts, the first row is worked in the direction of the arrow.

Lover's knot

This design can be used as an all-over pattern. Make a number of chain divisible by 132 plus 1 and 2 extra turning chain.

1st row Into 4th ch from hook work 1tr, 1tr into each of next 2ch, *(2ch, miss 2ch, 1tr into next ch) 5 times, 1tr into each of next 6ch, (2ch, miss 2ch, 1tr into next ch) 6 times, 1tr into each of next 6ch, (2ch, miss 2ch, 1tr into next ch) 5 times, 1tr into each of next 6ch, rep from * to end, ending with 1tr into each of last 3ch instead of 6ch. This row on the chart will read, *1 blk, 5 sps, 2 blks, 6 sps, 2 blks, 5 sps, 1 blk, rep from * to end.

2nd row 3ch to count as first tr, 1tr into each of next 3tr, *(2ch, 1tr into next tr) 5 times, 1tr into each of next 6tr, (2ch, 1tr into next tr) 6 times, 1tr into each of next 6tr, (2ch, 1tr into next tr) 5 times, 1tr into each of next 6tr, rep from * to end, ending with 1tr into each of next 2tr, 1tr into 3rd of first 3ch. This row on the chart is the same as the 1st row.

3rd row *9 sps, 4 blks, 9 sps, rep from * to end.

4th row *2 sps, 2 blks, 3 sps, 2 blks, 4 sps, 2 blks, 3 sps, 2 blks, 2 sps, rep from * to end.

Continue working from the chart, rep 42 rows as required. This pattern can be alternated for an all-over fabric, beginning alternate reps at point marked 'A' on chart.

Oak leaf insertion

Make 108ch.

1st row Into 4th ch from hook work 1tr, 1tr into each of next 2ch, (3ch, miss 2ch, 1dc into next ch, 3ch, miss 2ch, 1tr into next ch) twice, (2ch, miss 2ch, 1tr into next ch) 18 times, 1tr into each of next 3ch, (2ch, miss 2ch, 1tr into next ch) 6 times, (3ch, miss 2ch, 1dc into next ch, 3ch, miss 2ch, 1tr into next ch) twice, 1tr into each of next 3ch. This row on the chart will read, 1 blk, 2 lacets, 18 sps, 1 blk, 6 sps, 2 lacets, 1 blk.

2nd row 3ch to count as first tr, 1tr into each of next 3tr, (5ch, 1tr into next tr) twice, (2ch, 1tr into next tr) 6 times, 1tr into each of next 3tr, (2ch, 1tr into next tr) 18 times, (5ch, 1tr into next tr) twice, 1tr into each of next 2tr, 1tr into 3rd of first 5ch. This row on the chart will read 1 blk, 2 bars, 6 sps, 1 blk, 18 sps, 2 bars, 1 blk.

3rd row 3ch to count as first tr, 1tr into each of next 3tr, (3ch, 1dc into 3rd of 5ch, 3ch, 1tr into next tr) twice, (2ch, 1tr into next tr) 12 times, (2tr into next sp, 1tr into next tr) twice, (2ch, 1tr into next tr) 4 times, 1tr into each of next 3tr, (2ch, 1tr into next tr) 6 times, (3ch, 1dc into 3rd of 5ch, 3ch, 1tr into next tr) twice, 1tr into each of next 2tr, 1tr into 3rd of first 3ch. This row on the chart will read, 1 blk, 2 lacets, 12 sps, 2 blks, 4 sps, 1 blk, 6 sps, 2 lacets, 1 blk.

4th row 1 blk, 2 bars, 6 sps, 1 blk, 3 sps, 4 blks, 1 sp, 4 blks, 6 sps, 2 bars, 1 blk.

Continue working from the chart, rep 42 patt rows as required.

Rose motif or insertion

Make 108ch.

1st row Into 4th ch from hook work 1tr, 1tr into each of next 2ch, *2ch, miss 2ch, 1tr into next ch, rep from * to last 3ch, 1tr into each of next 3ch. This row on the chart will read, 1 blk, 33 sps, 1 blk.

2nd row 3ch to count as first tr, 1tr into each of next 3tr, (2ch, 1tr into next tr) 10 times, 2tr into next sp, 1tr into next tr, (2ch, 1tr into next tr) 11 times, 2tr into next sp, 1tr into next tr, (2ch, 1tr into next tr) 10 times, 1tr into each of next 2tr, 1tr into 3rd of first 3ch. This row on the chart will read, 1 blk, 10 sps, 1 blk, 11 sps, 1 blk, 10 sps, 1 blk.

3rd row 3ch to count as first tr, 1tr into each of next 3tr, (2ch, 1tr into next tr) 9 times, 2tr into next sp, 1tr into next tr, 2ch, miss 2tr, 1tr into next tr, (2ch, 1tr into next tr) 11 times, 2ch, miss 2tr, 1tr into next tr, 2tr into next sp, 1tr into next tr, (2ch, 1tr into next tr) 9 times, 1tr into each of next 2tr, 1tr into 3rd of first 3ch. This row on the chart will read, 1 blk, 9 sps, 1 blk, 13 sps, 1 blk, 9 sps, 1 blk.

4th row 1 blk, 9 sps, 4 blks, 9 sps, 1 blk, 1 sp, 1 blk, 8 sps, 1 blk.

Continue working from chart, rep 2nd to 41st rows to form patt.

A

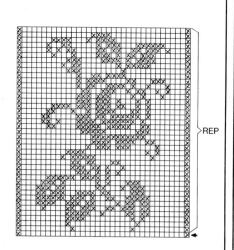

REP

Butterfly motif

Make 75ch.

1st row Into 4th ch from hook work 1tr, 1tr into each ch to end. 73tr.

2nd row 3ch to count as first tr, 1tr into each of next 3tr, (2ch, miss 2tr, 1tr into next tr) 22 times, 1tr into each of next 2tr, 1tr into 3rd of first 3ch. 1 blk, 22 sps and 1 blk.

3rd row 3ch to count as first tr, 1tr into each of next 3tr, (2ch, 1tr into next tr) 4 times, 2tr into next sp, 1tr into next tr, (2ch, 1tr into next tr) 9 times, 2tr into next sp, 1tr into next tr, (2ch, 1tr into next tr) 5 times, 2tr into next sp, 1tr into next tr, 2ch, 1tr into each of next 3tr, 1tr into 3rd of first 3ch. This row on the chart will read, 1 blk, 4 sps, 1 blk, 9 sps, 1 blk, 5 sps, 1 blk, 1 sp, 1 blk.

4th row Reading from the chart, 1 blk, 6 sps, 3 blks, 8 sps, 3 blks, 2 sps, 1 blk. Continue working from the chart.

Acorn pattern

This design can be used as an all-over pattern. Make a number of chain divisible by 36 plus 11, e.g. 83ch.

1st row Into 8th ch from hook work 1tr, *2ch, miss 2ch, 1tr into next ch, rep from * to end. Multiples of 12 sps plus 2.

2nd row 5ch to count as first tr and 2ch, *1tr into next tr, 2ch, rep from * to end, 1tr into 5th of first 7ch.

3rd row 5ch to count as first tr and 2ch, (1tr into next tr, 2ch) 8 times, *(1tr into next tr, 2tr into next sp) 3 times, (1tr into next tr, 2ch) 9 times, rep from * to last 5 sts, (1tr into next tr, 2tr into next sp) 3 times, (1tr into next tr, 2ch) twice, 1tr into 3rd of first 5ch. This row on the chart will read, *9 sps, 3 blocks, rep from * to last 2 sps, 2 sps.

4th row 2 sps, *4 blks, 8 sps, rep from * to end. Continue working from the chart, rep 2nd to 13th rows to form the patt.

Star motif

Make 62ch.

1st row Into 8th ch from hook work 1tr, *2ch, miss 2ch, 1tr into next ch, rep from * to end. 19 sps.

2nd row 5ch to count as first tr and 2ch, (1tr into next tr, 2ch) 4 times, 1tr into next tr, 2tr into next sp, (1tr into next tr, 2ch) 7 times, 1tr into next tr, 2tr into next sp, (1tr into next tr, 2ch) 5 times, 1tr into 5th of first 7ch. This row on the chart will read, 5 sps, 1 blk, 7 sps, 1 blk, 5 sps.

3rd row 5ch to count as first tr and 2ch, (1tr into next tr, 2ch) 4 times, 1tr into each of next 4tr, 2tr into next sp, (1tr into next tr, 2ch) 5 times, 1tr into next tr, 2tr into next sp, 1tr into each of next 4tr, (2ch, 1tr into next tr) 5 times working last tr into 3rd of first 5ch. This row on the chart will read, 5 sps, 2 blks, 7 sps, 2 blks, 5 sps.

4th row 5 sps, 3 blks, 3 sps, 3 blks, 5 sps. Continue working from the chart.

*From top to bottom: Lover's knot;
Oak leaf insertion; Rose motif;
Butterfly motif; Acorn pattern;
Star motif.*

53

Patchwork slip-on

Sizes

To fit 81.5/86.5 [91.5/96.5]cm (32/34[36/38]in) bust
Length to shoulder, 58.5[59.5]cm (23[23½]in)
The figures in brackets [] refer to the 91.5/96.5cm (36/38in) size only

Tension

24 sts and 12 rows to 10cm (3.9in) over tr worked on No.3.00 (ISR) crochet hook

Materials

1 x 50 grm ball each of Jaeger Celtic-Spun 4 ply in 6 contrast colours, A, B, C, D, E and F
One No.3.00 (ISR) crochet hook

Note

Slip-on is made in 10 separate panels. Twist yarns at back of work and change colours as given in Chapter 10

Slip-on

1st patch

Using No.3.00 (ISR) hook and A, make 22[24]ch.
1st row (RS) Into 4th ch from hook work 1tr, 1tr into each ch to end. 20[22]tr.
2nd row 3ch to count as first tr, 1tr into each tr to end.
Break off A. Rep 2nd row 10 times more, working 2 rows each in B, C, D, E and F. These 12 rows form 1st patch.

2nd patch

Using No.3.00 (ISR) hook and A, make 22[24]ch.
Work 1st and 2nd rows as given for 1st patch. Using A only, rep 2nd row 10 times more. These 12 rows form 2nd patch, varying colours as required for each subsequent rep of this patch.

3rd patch

Using No.3.00 (ISR) hook and C, make 22[24]ch. Work 1st and 2nd rows as given for 1st patch. Rep 2nd row 4 times more. Break off C. Join in D.
7th row Using D, 3ch to count as first tr, 1tr into each of next 9[10]tr, join in E on last tr, using E, 1tr into each of next 10[11]tr.
8th row Using E, 3ch to count as first tr, 1tr into each of next 9[10]tr, join in D on last tr, using D, 1tr into each of next 10[11]tr.
Rep 7th and 8th rows twice more. These 12 rows form 3rd patch.

4th patch

Using No.3.00 (ISR) hook and B, make 10[11]ch, join in F on last ch, using F, make 12[13]ch.
1st row Using F, into 4th ch from hook work 1tr, 1tr into each of next 8[9]ch, join in B on last ch, using B, 1tr into each of next 10[11]ch. 20[22]tr.
2nd row Using B and F, work as given for 8th row of 3rd patch.
Rep these 2 rows 5 times more. These 12 rows form 4th patch.

5th patch

Using No.3.00 (ISR) hook and A, make 22[24]ch. Work 1st and 2nd rows as given for 1st patch.

Rep 2nd row 3 times more. Break off A. Join in E. Rep 2nd row twice more. Break off E. Join in C. Rep 2nd row 5 times more. These 12 rows form 5th patch.

Centre front and back panels

Using colours and patches as required, work 48 continuous patt rows. Fasten off. Work 3 more panels in same way.

Underarm panels

Using colours and patches as required, work as given for centre panels. Work 1 more panel in same way.

Shoulder panels

Using colours and patches as required, work 70[72] continuous patt rows. Fasten off. Work 3 more panels in same way.

To make up

Press each panel under a damp cloth with a warm iron. Join panels as shown in diagram.

Edging Using No.3.00 (ISR) hook, any colour and with RS of work facing, work 3 rounds dc round lower edge. Work in same way round neck and armholes, dec one st in each corner on every round. Press edging.

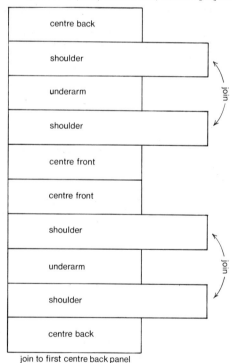

Cosy slip-on worked in simple strips of colourful patchwork crochet. The diagram (above) shows how the strips are joined to form a one-piece garment.

Edgings

Edging No.1
Make 14ch.

1st row (WS) Into 8th ch from hook work 1tr, 2ch, miss 2ch, work (2tr, 2ch, 2tr) into next ch, 2ch, miss 2ch, 1tr into last ch.

2nd row 5ch to count as first tr and 2ch, miss first 2ch sp, work (2tr, 2ch, 2tr) into next 2ch sp, 1tr into each of next 2tr, 2ch, 1tr into next tr, 2ch, 1tr into 5th of first 7ch.

3rd row 5ch, miss first tr, 1tr into next tr, 2ch, 1tr into each of next 4tr, wotk (2tr, 2ch, 2tr) into 2ch sp, 2ch, 1tr into 3rd of first 5ch.

4th row 5ch to count as first tr and 2ch, miss first 2ch sp, work (2tr, 2ch, 2tr) into next 2ch sp, 1tr into each of next 6tr, 2ch, 1tr into next tr, 2ch, 1tr into 5ch loop, work (2ch, 1tr) 6 times into same loop, 2ch, ss into base of tr at end of 2nd row, turn.

5th row 5ch, 1dc into first 2ch sp, work (1dc, 5ch, 1dc) into each of next seven 2ch sps, 3ch, 1tr into first tr of 8tr gr, 2ch, miss 3tr, 1tr into next tr, 2ch, work (2tr, 2ch, 2tr) into next 2ch sp, 2ch, 1tr into 3rd of first 5ch.

The 2nd to 5th rows form the pattern, ending 2nd rows by working last tr into 1st tr of previous row.

Edging No.2
Make 19ch.

1st row (RS) Into 3rd ch from hook work 1htr, 1htr into each ch to end. 18 sts.

2nd row 4ch to count as first dtr, *yrh 3 times, insert hook into next htr and draw a loop through, (yrh and draw through 2 loops) twice, (3 loops on hook), yrh, miss 2htr, insert hook into next htr and draw a loop through, (yrh and draw through 2 loops on hook) 4 times, (1 loop on hook), 2ch, 1tr into centre point of cross just made, rep from * 3 times more, 1dtr into 2nd of first 2ch.

3rd row 2ch to count as first htr, *1htr into next st, 2htr into 2ch sp, 1htr into next st, rep from * to end, 1htr into 4th of first 4ch.
Rep 2nd and 3rd rows for the required length, ending with a 3rd row. Do not break off yarn but turn work sideways and work along edge, as foll:

1st row 1ch, 1dc into edge of htr, *4dc into 4ch edge, 2dc into edge of next htr, rep from * to end.

2nd row 6ch to count as first dtr and 2ch, miss edge st and next dc, *work a cross st as on 2nd row of edging over next 4dc, 2ch, miss 2dc, rep from * to end, ending with miss 1dc, 1dtr into first 1ch. Note that the cross sts should come over the 4dc worked into the 4ch each time.

3rd row 5ch, 1dc into first leg of cross, 5ch, 1dc into next leg of cross, rep from * to end, ending with 5ch, 1dc into 4th of first 6ch.
Fasten off.

Edging No.3
Make a number of chain diviisble by 27 plus 25 and 4 extra turning chain.

1st row (RS) Into 8th ch from hook work 1tr, *2ch, miss 2ch, 1tr into next ch, rep from * to end. This makes a number of tr divisible by 9, or sps divisible by 9 plus 8.

2nd row 5ch to count as first tr and 2ch, miss first tr and 2ch, 1tr into next tr, *2ch, 1tr into next tr, rep from * to end working last tr into 5th of first 7ch.

3rd row 4ch, keeping last loop of each dtr on hook work 2dtr into the first tr (edge st), yrh and draw through all 3 loops on hook, *4ch, miss 1tr, work (1tr, 2ch, 1tr) into next tr, 4ch, miss 1tr, work (1dtr, 3ch, 1dtr) into next tr, 4ch, miss 1tr, work (1tr, 2ch, 1tr) into next tr, 4ch, miss 1tr, keeping last loop of each dtr on hook work 3dtr into next tr, yrh and draw through all 4 loops on hook — called 1Cl or cluster —, 2ch, 1Cl into next tr, rep from * to end omitting last 2ch and 1Cl and working last 1Cl into 3rd of first 5ch.

4th row 4ch, keeping last loop of each dtr on hook work 2dtr into top of first 1Cl at edge, yrh and draw through all 3 loops on hook, *4ch, work (1tr, 2ch, 1tr) into next 2ch sp, 4ch, work (1dtr, 3ch, 1dtr) into next 3ch sp, 4ch, work (1tr, 2ch, 1tr) into 2ch sp, 4ch, 1Cl into top of 1Cl, 2ch, 1Cl into top of next 1Cl, rep from * to end omitting last 2ch and 1Cl.

5th row 1ch to count as first dc, *2ch, work (1tr, 2ch, 1tr) into 2ch sp, 4ch, work (1dtr, 3ch, 1dtr) into next 3ch sp, 4ch, work (1dtr, 3ch, 1dtr) into next 3ch sp, 4ch, work (1tr, 2ch, 1tr) into next 2ch sp, 2ch, 1dc into top of 1Cl, 2dc into 2ch sp between Cl, 1dc into top of next 1Cl, rep from * to end omitting last 3dc.

6th row 1ch to count as first dc, *2ch, work (1tr, 2ch, 1tr) into 2ch sp between tr, 5ch, work (1dtr, 3ch, 1dtr) into next 3ch sp, 4ch, work (1dtr, 3ch, 1dtr) into next 4ch sp, 4ch, work (1dtr, 3ch, 1dtr) into next 3ch sp, 5ch, work (1tr, 2ch, 1tr) into next 2ch sp, 2ch, miss 1dc, 1dc into each of next 2dc, rep from * to end, ending with 2ch, 1dc into first ch.

7th row 1ch to count as first dc, *work (1tr, 2ch, 1tr) into 2ch sp between tr, (5ch, 5tr into next 3ch sp) 3 times, 5ch, work (1tr, 2ch, 1tr) into next 2ch sp, miss next 2ch sp, 2dc and 2ch sp, rep from * to end, ending with (1tr, 2ch, 1tr) into 2ch sp, 1dc into first ch. Fasten off.

Edging No.4
Make 14ch.

1st row (RS) Into 7th ch from hook work 1tr, 2ch, 1tr into next ch, 3ch, miss 2ch, 1dc into next ch, 3ch, miss 2ch, work (1tr, 2ch, 1tr) into last ch.

2nd row 3ch to count as first tr, 2ch, 1tr into first 2ch sp, 3ch, 5tr into next 2ch sp, turn.

3rd row 5ch, miss first 2tr, work (1tr, 2ch, 1tr) into next tr, 3ch, 1dc into 2nd of next 3ch, 3ch, **4th row** 3ch to count as first tr, 2ch, 1tr into first 2ch sp, 3ch, 5tr into next 2ch sp, 3ch, 1tr into 5ch loop, (2ch, 1tr) 4 times into same 5ch loop, 3ch, miss next row end, 1ss into 3rd of 6ch at beg of 1st row, turn.

5th row 1ch to count as first dc, 3dc into 3ch sp, work (1dc, 3ch, 1dc) into each of next four 2ch sps, 3dc into next 3ch sp, 3ch, miss 2tr, work work (1tr, 2ch, 1tr) into 2ch sp at end.

(1tr, 2ch, 1tr) into next tr, 3ch, 1dc into 2nd of 3ch, 3ch, work (1tr, 2ch, 1tr) into 2ch sp at end.
The 2nd to 5th rows form the pattern, noting that when working a repeat of the 4th row, the last ss is worked into the dc before the 3ch loop of the previous 5th row.

Edging No.5
Make 8ch.

1st row (RS) Into 8th ch from hook work (2tr, 3ch, 2tr), turn.

2nd row 9ch, work (2tr, 10ch, 2tr) into 3ch sp, turn.

3rd row 5ch, work 17tr into 10ch sp, 1dc into 9ch loop, turn.

4th row (5ch, miss 1tr, 1dc into next tr) 5 times, turn.

5th row 7ch, work (2tr, 3ch, 2tr) into first 5ch loop, turn.

Rep the 2nd to 5th rows for the required length, ending with a 4th row. Do not break off yarn but turn work sideways and work along edge, as foll:

1st row 7ch, 1dc into next 5ch loop, 5ch, keeping last loop of each tr on hook work 3tr into next 7ch loop, yrh and draw through all 4 loops on hook — called 1Cl or cluster —, *5ch, 1dc into next 5ch loop, 5ch, 1Cl into next 7ch loop, rep from * to end working last 1Cl into commencing 7ch loop.

2nd row 3ch to count as first tr, work 6tr into each 5ch loop to end, 6tr into first 7ch loop, turn.

3rd row 4ch to count as first tr and 1ch, miss first 2tr, 1tr into next tr, *1ch, miss 1tr, 1tr into next tr, rep from * to end. Fasten off.

Edging No.6
Make 10ch. Join with a ss to first ch to form circle.

1st row (WS) 3ch to count as first tr, 14tr into circle, turn.

2nd row 5ch to count as first tr and 2ch, miss edge st and next tr, 1tr into next tr, *2ch, miss 1tr, 1tr into next tr, rep from * 5 times more, working last tr into 3rd of first 3ch.

3rd row *3ch, 7tr into next 2ch sp, take hook out of last working loop and insert from front to back into 3rd of 3ch, then into the working loop and draw the loop through, rep from * 6 times more, turn.

4th row 10ch, miss two 3ch sp, work (1dc, 5ch, 1dc) into next 3ch sp, turn.

5th row 3ch to count as first tr, 13tr into 5ch loop, 1dc into 10ch loop, turn.

Rep the 2nd to 5th rows for the required length, ending with a 3rd row. Do not break off yarn but turn work sideways and work as foll:

Next row *10ch, 1dc into next 10ch loop, 5ch, 1dc into 3rd of 3ch at beg of next row, rep from * to end. Fasten off.

Edging No. 1

Edging No. 2

Edging No. 3

Edging No. 4

Edging No. 5

Edging No. 6

Edging No. 7

Edging No. 8

Edging No.7

Make 21ch.

1st row (WS) Into 8th ch from hook work 1tr, (2ch, miss 2ch, 1tr into next ch) 3 times, 5ch, miss 3ch, 1tr into last ch, (3ch, 1tr into same ch) 3 times, turn.

2nd row Into each of three 3ch loops work (1dc, 1htr, 1tr, 1dtr, 1tr, 1htr, 1dc—called 1 shamrock), 5ch, 1tr into 5ch sp, (2ch, 1tr into next tr) 4 times, 2ch, 1tr into 5th of first 7ch.

3rd row 5ch to count as first tr and 2ch, 1tr into next tr, (2ch, 1tr into next tr) 4 times, 2ch, 1tr into 5ch sp, 7ch, 1tr into dtr in centre of shamrock, (3ch, 1tr into same dtr) 3 times, turn.

4th row Make a shamrock as on 2nd row, 5ch, 1tr into 7ch loop, (2ch, 1tr into next tr) 6 times, 2ch, 1tr into 5th of first 7ch.

5th row As 3rd but work (2ch, 1tr into next tr) 6 times instead of 4 times.

6th row As 4th but working (2ch, 1tr into next tr)

8 times instead of 6 times.

7th row 5ch to count as first tr and 2ch, miss first tr and 2ch, 1tr into next tr, (2ch, 1tr into next tr) 3 times, 7ch, miss four 2ch sp, 1tr into next 2ch sp, (3ch, 1tr into same sp) 3 times, turn.

Rep the 2nd to 7th rows for the required length, ending with a 6th row.

Edging No.8

Make 53ch.

1st row (RS) Into 8th ch from hook work 1tr, 2ch, miss 2ch, 1tr into each of next 4ch, (2ch, miss 2ch, 1tr into next ch) 5 times, 1tr into each of next 12ch, (2ch, miss 2ch, 1tr into each of next 4ch) twice. This row on the chart will read, 2 sps, 1 blk, 5 sps, 4 blks, 1 sp, 1blk, 1 sp, 1 blk.

2nd row 3ch to count as first tr, 1tr into each of next 3tr, 2ch, 1tr into next tr, 2ch, miss 2tr,

1tr into next tr, 2tr into sp, 1tr into next tr, (2ch, miss 2tr, 1tr into next tr) twice, 1tr into each of next 6tr, 2tr into sp, 1tr into next tr, (2ch, 1tr into next tr) 4 times, 1tr into each of next 3tr, 2ch, 1tr into next tr, 2ch, 1tr into 5th of first 7ch. This row on the chart will read, 1 blk, 2 sps, 1 blk, 2 sps, 3 bks, 4 sps, 1 blk, 2 sps.

3rd row 7ch, 1tr into first tr (edge st) — one sp inc —, then work 1 sp, 1 blk, 9 sps, 1 blk, 1 sp, 1 blk, 1 sp, 1 blk.

4th row 1 blk, 1 sp, 1 blk, 2 sps, 1 blk, 3 sps, 4 blks, 2 sps, 1 blk, 1 sp working last tr of this sp into 5th of first 7ch of 1st row, 5ch, 1tr into same place as last tr, turn and work 1ss into each of the first 3ch — 1 sp inc.

Beg with a 5th row cont in patt from chart, inc 1 sp at end of 6th row as given in 4th row. To dec at end of 12th and 14th rows, work to last sp, turn, and to dec 1 sp at beg of 15th (or 1st) row, ss over first sp, 5ch to count as first tr and 2ch, cont in patt to end.

Edging No.9

Make 150ch and work in patt from chart, working 1st row from A to B, as foll:

1st row Into 4th ch from hook work 1tr, 1tr into each of next 2ch, (2ch, miss 2ch, 1tr into next ch) 29 times, 1tr into each of next 3ch, (2ch, miss 2ch, 1tr into next ch) 17 times, 1tr into each of next 3ch. 1 blk, 29 sps, 1 blk, 17 sps 1 blk.

2nd row 1 blk, 18 sps, 2 blks, 6 sps, 3 blks, 18 sps, 1 blk.

Cont in patt from chart until 55th row has been worked, shown as C on chart.

56th row Patt to last 2 sps, turn.

57th row Patt to end.

58th row Patt to last 2 sps, turn.

Cont to dec 2 sps or blks on every alt row until 101st row has been worked, noting that this row will read, 2 sps, 1 blk.

Next row 1 blk, turn.

Next row 1 blk, ending at outside edge, turn and ss across the 4tr of this blk to inside edge.

Turn work through 90 degrees and cont along 2nd side, beg at point marked D on chart.

1st row 3ch, 3tr into side of last blk, 2ch, ss into the tr between 2 sps on 101st row.

2nd row Ss over the next 3ch of first sp on 101st row, turn and cont back along row just worked, 1 sp, 1 blk, turn.

3rd row 2 blks, 2 sps, ss into tr between sps on 99th row.

4th row Ss over the next 3ch of first sp on 99th

row, turn and cont back along row just worked, 1 sp, 3 blks, turn.

5th row 4 blks, 2 sps, ss into tr between sps on 97th row.

Cont in this way until 48 rows have been completed, ending at outside edge.

49th row Patt to end, then work 3tr into side of blk on 55th row at point marked C on chart.

This completes corner shaping. Cont in patt from chart until 151st row has been completed, point marked EF, then beg again at point marked AB. If a longer edging is required the rep of the patt is from row 70 on the side after the corner to row 30 on the first side, 122 rows in all.

Edging No. 9

Edging No. 8

57

Aran patterns

Aran rib
Make the required number of chain and 1 extra turning chain.
1st row (RS) Into 3rd ch from hook work 1htr, 1htr into each ch to end.
2nd row 2ch to count as first htr, miss first htr, work 1htr into horizontal loop in front of each htr to end, 1htr into 2nd of first 2ch.
3rd row 2ch to count as first htr, miss first htr, work 1htr into back loop only of each htr to end, 1htr into 2nd of first 2ch.
The 2nd and 3rd rows form the pattern.

Mock cable pattern
Make a number of chain divisible by 6 plus 2 and 2 extra turning chain.
1st row (WS) Into 4th ch from hook work 1tr, 1tr into each ch to end.
2nd row 3ch to count as first tr, miss first tr, 1tr into next tr, *miss 2tr, 1dtr into each of next 2tr, keeping hook at back of work work 1dtr into each of the 2 missed tr, 1tr into each of next 2tr, rep from * to end working last tr into 3rd of first 3ch.
3rd row 3ch to count as first tr, miss 1tr, 1tr into next tr, *miss 2dtr, 1dtr into each of next 2dtr, keeping hook at front of work work 1dtr into each of the 2 missed dtr, 1tr into each of next 2tr, rep from * to end working last tr into 3rd of first 3ch.
4th row As 2nd but working the dtr into dtr of 3rd row.
The 3rd and 4th rows form the pattern.

Cable panel
Worked over 17 stitches and 1 stitch at each end. Make 20 chain.
1st row (RS) Into 3rd ch from hook work 1htr, 1htr into each ch to end.
2nd row 2ch to count as first htr, miss first htr, work 1htr into each htr to end working last htr into 2nd of first 2ch.
3rd row 2ch to count as first htr, miss first htr, *work 1RtF round each of next 2htr, see Chapter 15, 1htr into next htr, rep from * to end working last htr into 2nd of first 2ch.
4th and every alt row 2ch to count as first htr, miss first htr, 1htr into each st to end working last htr into 2nd of first 2ch.
5th row 2ch to count as first htr, miss first htr, (1RtF round each of next 2RtF on 3rd row, 1htr into next htr) twice, (miss next 2RtF and 1htr, yrh twice, insert hook round stem of next RtF from front to back and complete as for dtr — called RdtF —, 1RdtF into next RtF, keeping hook at back of work 1htr into the missed htr, then keeping hook in front of work but *behind* the 2RdtF just worked, work 1RdtF into each of the 2 missed RtF — called Cr5B —), (1htr into next htr, 1RtF round each of next 2RtF) twice, 1htr into next htr, rep from * to end working last htr into 2nd of first 2ch.
7th row 2ch to count as first htr, miss first htr, work 1RtF round each of next 2RtF, 1htr into next htr, (miss 2RtF and next 1htr, work 1RdtF round each of next 2RtF, keeping hook at back of work 1htr into the missed htr, then keeping hook at front of work and *in front* of the 2RdtF just worked, work 1RdtF round each of the 2 missed RtF — called Cr5F —), 1htr into next htr, Cr5F, 1htr into next htr, 1RtF round each of next 2RrF, 1htr into 2nd of first 2ch.
9th row 2ch to count as first htr, miss first htr, (Cr5B, 1htr into next htr) twice, Cr5B, 1htr into 2nd of first 2ch.
11th row As 7th.
13th row As 5th.
15th and 17th rows As 3rd but working RtF round RtF and not round htr.
18th row As 4th.
The 5th to 18th rows form the pattern.

Lattice panel
Worked over 26 stitches. Make 27 chain.
1st row (RS) Into 3rd ch from hook work 1htr, 1htr into each ch to end.
2nd row 2ch to count as first htr, miss first htr, 1htr into each htr to end working last htr into 2nd of first 2ch.
3rd row 2ch to count as first htr, miss first htr, 1htr into next htr, work 1RtF round each of next 2htr, see Chapter 15, 1htr into each of next 2htr, rep from * to end working last htr into 2nd of first 2ch.
4th and every alt row 2ch to count as first htr, miss first htr, 1htr into each st to end working last htr into 2nd of first 2ch.
5th row 2ch to count as first htr, miss first htr, 1htr into next htr, *(miss 2RtF and 2htr, work 1RdtF round each of next 2RtF, see cable panel, keeping hook at back of work 1htr into each of the 2 missed htr, then keeping hook at front of work and *in front* of the 2RdtF just worked, work 1RdtF round each of the 2 missed RtF — called Cr6F —), 1htr into each of next 2htr, rep from * to end working last htr into 2nd of first 2ch.
7th row 2ch to count as first htr, miss first htr, 1htr into next htr, 1RtF round each of next 2RdtF, *1htr into each of next 2htr, (miss 2RdtF and 2htr, work 1RdtF round each of the next 2RdtF, keeping hook at back of work 1htr into each of the 2 missed htr, then keeping hook in front of work but *behind* the 2RdtF just worked, work 1RdtF round each of the 2 missed RdtF — called Cr6B —), rep from * once more, 1htr into each of next 2htr, 1RtF round each of next 2RdtF, 1htr into next htr, 1htr into 2nd of first 2ch.
9th row As 5th, reading RdtF instead of RtF where appropriate.
10th row As 4th.
The 7th to 10th rows form the pattern.

Diamond panel
Worked over 14 stitches. Make 15 chain.
1st row (RS) Into 3rd ch from hook work 1dc, 1dc into each ch to end.
2nd row 1ch to count as first dc, miss first dc, 1dc into each dc to end working last dc into 2nd of first 2ch.
3rd row 1ch to count as first dc, miss first dc, 1dc into next dc, 1RtF round next dc on 1st row, see Chapter 15, miss the same 1dc on 2nd row, 1dc into each of next 8dc, 1RtF round next dc on 1st row, miss the same 1dc on 2nd row, 1dc into next dc, 1dc into first ch.
4th and every alt row 1ch to count as first dc, miss first dc, 1dc into each st to end working last dc into first ch.
5th row 1ch to count as first dc, miss first dc, 1dc into each of next 2dc, 1RtF round next RtF, miss 1dc, 1dc into each of next 6dc, 1RtF round next RtF, miss 1dc, 1dc into each of next 2dc, 1dc into first ch.
7th row 1ch to count as first dc, miss first dc, 1dc into each of next 3dc, 1RtF round next RtF, miss 1dc, 1dc into each of next 4dc, 1RtF round next RtF, miss 1dc, 1dc into each of next 3dc, 1dc into first ch.
9th row 1ch to count as first dc, miss first dc, 1dc into each of next 4dc, 1RtF round next RtF, miss 1dc, 1dc into each of next 2dc, 1RtF round next RtF, miss 1dc, 1dc into each of next 4dc, 1dc into first ch.
11th row 1ch to count as first dc, miss first dc, 1dc into each of next 5dc, 1RtF round each of next 2RtF, miss 2dc, 1dc into each of next 5dc, 1dc into first ch.
13th row 1ch to count as first dc, 1dc into each of next 5dc, miss 1RtF, 1RtF round next RtF, 1RtF round the missed RtF, miss 2dc, 1dc into each of next 5dc, 1dc into first ch.
15th row As 9th.
17th row As 7th.
19th row As 5th.
21st row 1ch to count as first dc, miss first dc, 1dc into next dc, 1RtF round next RtF, miss 1dc, 1dc into each of next 8dc, 1RtF round next RtF, miss 1dc, 1dc into next dc, 1dc into first ch.
22nd row As 4th.
The 5th to 22nd rows form the pattern.

Chevron pattern
Make a number of chain divisible by 6 plus 2 and 1 extra turning chain.
1st row (RS) Into 3rd ch from hook work 1dc, 1dc into each ch to end.
2nd row 1ch to count as first dc, miss first dc, 1dc into each dc to end working last dc into 2nd of first 2ch.
3rd and 4th rows As 2nd working last dc into first ch.
5th row 1ch to count as first dc, miss first dc, 1dc into each of next 2dc, 1RtF round 2nd dc of 2nd row, see Chapter 15, *miss 4dc on 2nd row, 1RtF round next dc on 2nd row, miss 2dc on 4th row, 1dc into each of next 4dc on 4th row, 1RtF round dc on 2nd row next to last RtF, rep from * to last 5 sts on 4th row, miss 4dc on 2nd row, 1RtF round next dc on 2nd row, miss 2dc on 4th row, 1dc into next dc on 4th row, 1dc into first ch.
The 2nd to 5th rows form the pattern.

Aran rib

Chevron pattern

Mock cable pattern

Cable panel

Lattice panel

Diamond panel

Tunisian crochet stitches

Simple two-colour pattern
Using A, make the required number of chains.
1st row As 1st row of basic Tunisian stitch, see Chapter 14. Join in B.

Slip stitch pattern in two colours
Using A, make a odd number of chain.
1st row As 1st row of basic Tunisian stitch, see Chapter 14. Join in B.
2nd row Using B, as 2nd row of basic Tunisian stitch.

Two-colour check pattern
Using A, make a number of chain divisible by 6 plus 3.
1st row Using A, insert hook into 2nd ch from hook and draw a loop through, insert hook into next ch and draw a loop through ,*using B, (insert hook into next ch and draw a loop through)

Two-coloured mock rib
Using A, make an even number of chain and work 1st row as given for basic Tunisian stitch, see Chapter 14. Join in B.
2nd row Using B, as 2nd row of basic Tunisian stitch.
3rd row Using B, *insert hook from right to left behind vertical thread of next st and draw a loop through, insert hook from left to right behind vertical thread of next st and draw a loop through, rep from * to last st, insert hook into last st and draw a loop through. Change to A.
4th row Using A, as 2nd.
5th row Using A, *insert hook from left to right behind vertical thread of next st and draw a loop through, insert hook from right to left behind vertical thread of next st and draw a loop through, rep from * to last st, insert hook into last st and draw a loop through. Change to B.
6th row As 2nd.
The 3rd to 6th rows form the pattern.

2nd row Using B, as 2nd row of basic Tunisian stitch.
3rd row Using B, as 3rd row of basic Tunisian stitch. Change to A.

3rd row Using B, *insert hook behind vertical thread of next st and draw up a loop, yfwd, insert hook behind vertical thread of next st and sl it on to the hook without drawing up a loop — called sl 1 —, ybk, rep from * to last 2 sts, draw up a loop on each of last 2 sts. Change to A.

3 times, using A, (insert hook into next ch and draw a loop through) 3 times, rep from * to end.
2nd row As 2nd row of basic Tunisian stitch, see Chapter 14, working 3 sts in A, *3 sts in B, 3 sts in A, rep from * to end.
3rd row As 3rd row of basic Tunisian stitch, working 3 sts in A, *3 sts in B, 3 sts in A, rep

Brick pattern
Using A, make a number of chain divisible by 4 plus 1. Work first 2 rows of basic Tunisian stitch, see Chapter 14, joining in B on last st of 2nd row, see Chapter 9.
3rd and 4th rows Using B, work in basic Tunisian stitch. Change to A on last st of 4th row.
5th row Using A, insert hook behind vertical thread of next st and draw a loop through, *yrh,

Two-colour wave pattern
Using A, make a number of chain divisible by 10 plus 2. Work first 2 rows of basic Tunisian stitch, see Chapter 14, joining in B on last stitch of 2nd row, see Chapter 9.
3rd row Using B, insert hook from right to left behind vertical thread of next st and sl it on to the hook — called 1 sl st —, *work 2 basic stitches, work 4tr (see Chapter 14), 2 basic stitches, 2 sl sts, rep from * to end.
4th row Using B, as 2nd row of basic Tunisian stitch. Change to A on last st.
5th and 6th rows Using A, work in basic pattern. Change to B on last st.
7th row Using B, 1ch, work 1tr into each of next 2 sts, *2 basic stitches, 2 sl sts, 2 basic sts, 4tr, rep from * to end, ending with 3tr instead of 4tr.
8th row As 4th.
9th and 10th rows As 5th and 6th rows.
The 3rd to 10th rows form the pattern, ending with a 6th or 10th row.

4th row Using A, as 2nd row.
The 3rd and 4th rows form the pattern, working 2 rows in each colour throughout and always changing colour to work the even numbered rows.

4th row Using A, as 2nd row.
5th row Using A, *yfwd, sl 1, ybk, draw up a loop in next st, rep from * to end. Change to B.
The 2nd to 5th rows form the pattern, ending with a 2nd or 4th row.

from * to end.
4th row As 2nd.
5th to 8th rows As 3rd and 4th rows but reading A for B and B for A.
9th to 12th rows As 3rd and 4th rows.
The 5th to 12th rows form the pattern.

insert hook from right to left behind vertical threads of next st but on the row below (i.e. the 1st row) and draw a loop through, yrh and draw through 2 loops on hook — called 1 long tr —, draw a loop through each of next 3 sts in basic pattern, rep from * to end, ending with 1 long tr and 2 basic stitches.
6th row Using A, as 2nd row. Change to B on last st.

7th and 8th rows Using B, as 3rd and 4th rows. Change to A on last st.
9th row Using A, draw up a loop in each of next 3 sts, *1 long tr working into the 5th row, 3 basic stitches, rep from * to last st, 1 basic st in last st.
10th row As 6th.
The 3rd to 10th rows form the pattern, ending with a 6th or 10th row.

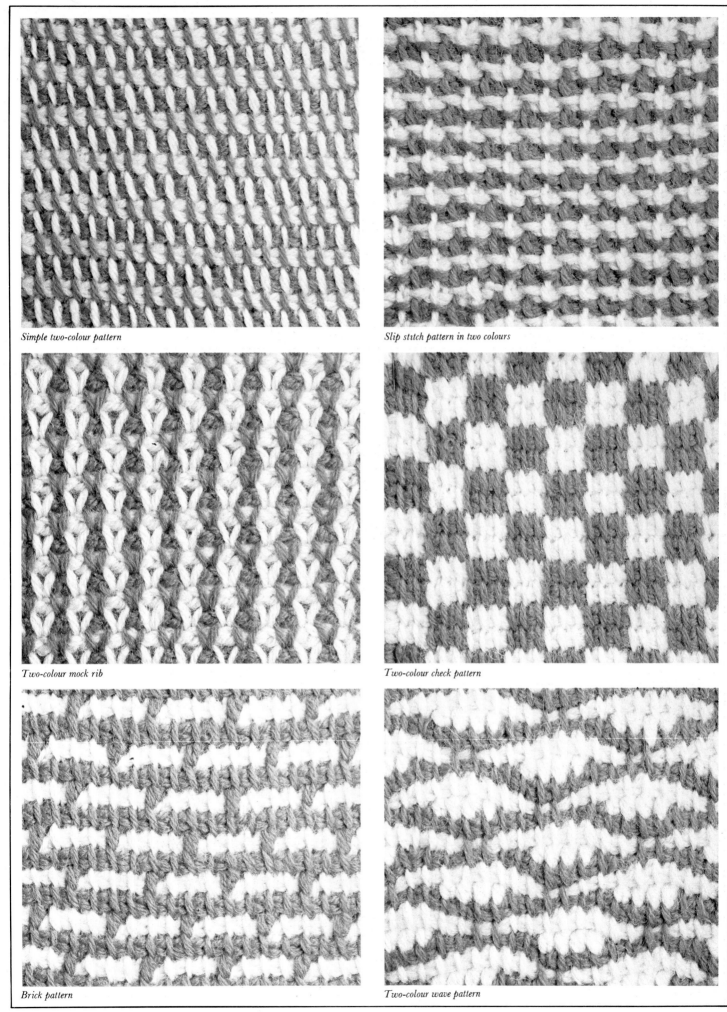

Simple two-colour pattern

Slip stitch pattern in two colours

Two-colour mock rib

Two-colour check pattern

Brick pattern

Two-colour wave pattern

61

Five simple designs

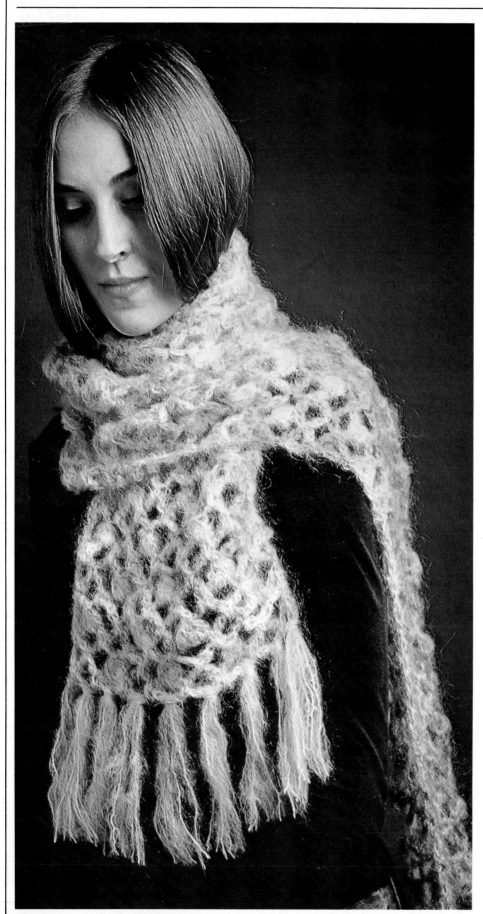

Mohair muffler
Size
25cm (9¾in) wide by 167.5cm (66in) long, adjustable
Tension
2 patts and 10 rows to 15cm (6in) worked on No.6.00 (ISR) crochet hook
Materials
6 x 25grm balls of Lister Tahiti or Lee Target Mohair
One No.6.00 (ISR) crochet hook

Muffler
Using No.6.00 (ISR) hook make 37ch. Work in mesh and cluster patt as given in Chapter 17, until work measures 167.5cm (66in), or required length, ending with a 3rd or 5th patt row. Fasten off. Trim each end with knotted fringe, if required.

Loopy tea-cosy
Size
23cm (9in) high by 32cm (12½in) wide
Tension
16 sts and 20 rows to 10cm (3.9in) over patt worked on No.4.00 (ISR) crochet hook
Materials
7 x 25grm balls of Wendy Random Double Knitting
One No.4.00 (ISR) crochet hook
Length of card 2cm (¾in) wide

Tea-cosy
Using No.4.00 (ISR) hook make 53ch.
1st row (RS) Into 3rd ch from hook work 1dc, 1dc into each ch to end. 52 sts.
2nd row 1ch to count as first dc, *holding strip of card at back of work, insert hook into next st so that it comes above the card, wind yarn towards you round the hook and the card twice, then round the hook again, draw this loop through the first 2 loops and the st, (2 loops on hook), yrh and draw through rem 2 loops, rep from * to end, moving the card along as necessary, ending with 1dc into 2nd of first 2ch.
3rd row 1ch to count as first dc, 1dc into each st to end, ending with 1dc into first ch.
4th row As 2nd, ending with 1dc into first ch.
Rep 3rd and 4th rows until work measures 15cm (6in) from beg, ending with a 4th row.
Shape top
Next row Ss over first 2 sts, 1ch, 1dc into each st to last 2 sts, turn.
Next row Patt to end.
Rep last 2 rows 3 times more. Dec in same way, dec 3 sts at each end of next and foll alt row, then 4 sts at each end of foll 2 alt rows, ending with a WS row. 8 sts. Fasten off. Make another piece in same way
To make up
Join 2 pieces tog. Cut 12 lengths of yarn 244cm (96in) long and make a twisted cord as given on page 11. St cord round seam, with a loop at top.

Crochet carpet bag
Size
38cm (15in) wide by 38cm (15in) deep
Tension
Each motif measures 12.5cm (5in) by 12.5cm (5in) worked on No. 4.00 (ISR) crochet hook
Materials
Approximately 10 x 25grm balls of Double Knitting yarn in assorted colours, or oddments

One No.4.00 (ISR) crochet hook
Pair of wooden handles 25.5cm (10in) across
lower edge

1st motif
Using No.4.00 (ISR) hook and any colour, make
8ch. Join with a ss to first ch to form circle.
1st round 3ch, (yrh, insert hook into circle and
draw a loop through, yrh and draw through 2
loops on hook) twice, yrh and draw through all 3
loops on hook, 2ch, work instructions in brackets
3 times more, yrh and draw through all 4 loops on
hook — called 1Cl —, (5ch, 1Cl, 2ch, 1Cl) 3
times, 5ch. Join with a ss to top of first Cl or 3rd
of first 3ch.
2nd round Ss into next 2ch sp, 3ch to count as
first tr, 2tr into same 2ch sp, 2ch, (1Cl, 3ch,
1Cl) into next 5ch sp, 2ch, *3tr into next 2ch
sp, 2ch (1Cl, 3ch, 1Cl) into 5ch sp, 2ch, rep from
* twice more. Join with a ss to 3rd of first 3ch.
3rd round 3ch to count as first tr, 1tr into each
of next 2tr, *2tr into 2ch sp, 2ch, (1Cl, 3ch, 1Cl)
into 3ch sp, 2ch, 2tr into 2ch sp, 1tr into each
of next 3tr, rep from * 3 times more, omitting
last 3tr. Join with a ss to 3rd of first 3ch.
4th round 3ch to count as first tr, 1tr into each
of next 4tr, *2tr into 2ch sp, 2ch, (1Cl, 3ch,
1Cl) into 3ch sp, 2ch, 2tr into 2ch sp, 1tr into
each of next 7tr, rep from * 3 times more, ending
with 1tr into each of last 2tr. Join with a ss to
3rd of first 3ch.
5th round 3ch to count as first tr, 1tr into each
of next 6tr, *2tr into 2ch sp, 2ch, (1Cl, 3ch,
1Cl) into 3ch sp, 2ch, 2tr into 2ch sp, 1tr into
each of next 11tr, rep from * 3 times more,
ending with 1tr into each of last 4tr. Join with a ss
to 3rd of first 3ch. Fasten off.
Using colours as required, make 17 more motifs
in same way.
To make up
Join 3 motifs to form each row, then join 6 rows.
Fold work in half and join 2 motifs at each side,
using dc through both thicknesses of 2 motifs,
then through one thickness of next motif, across
top edge and down first motif of other side, then
through both thicknesses of rem 2 motifs. Complete rem edges in dc. Fold top edge over handle
and sl st down.

Lampshade cover
Size
Approximately 25cm (9¾in) diameter by 19cm
(7½in) deep
Tension
14 V sts and 15 rows to 10cm (3.9in) worked on
No.1.50 (ISR) crochet hook
Materials
2 x 20 grm balls of Coat's Mercer-Crochet
No.20 for main section
2 x 20 grm balls of Coat's Mercer-Crochet
No.10 for edging and trimmings
One No.1.50 (ISR) crochet hook
Length of buckram or parchment for mounting

Lampshade
Using No.1.50 (ISR) hook and No. 20 cotton,
make 139ch and beg at top. Join with a ss to first
ch to form circle.
1st round 5ch, miss 1ch, 1tr into next ch, (2ch,
miss 1ch, 1tr into next ch) 68 times, miss 1ch,
2ch. Join with a ss to 3rd of first 5ch. 70 sps.
2nd round 5ch, 1tr into next tr, (2ch, 1tr into
next tr) 68 times, 2ch. Join with a ss to 3rd of
first 5ch.
3rd round 5ch, 1dtr into base of 5ch, (1dtr, 1ch,
1dtr) into each tr to end. Join with a ss to 4th
of first 5ch.
4th round 5ch, 1dtr into base of 5ch, (1dtr, 1ch,

Left: Warm, quick-to-make mohair muffler
Top right: Loopy tea-cosy, using scraps of yarn
Right: Capacious carpet bag made from motifs

1dtr) into ch sp between each dtr — called V st —, to end. Join with a ss to 4th of first 5ch.
Rep 4th round twice more.

7th round 6ch, 1dtr into base of 6ch, (1dtr, 2ch, 1dtr) into each V st to end. Join with a ss to 4th of first 6ch.
Rep 7th round 5 times more.

13th round (inc round) *Work 9 V st as 7th round, between next 2 V sts work a double V of (1dtr, 2ch, 1dtr, 2ch, 1dtr), rep from * to end. Join with a ss to 4th of first 6ch.

14th round Work 1 V st into each V st, working 1 V st into centre dtr of each double V st. Join as before.

Work 2 rounds V st without shaping.

17th round (inc round) *Work 10 V st, between next 2 V sts work a double V, rep from * to end. Join as before.

18th round As 14th.

Work 2 rounds V st without shaping.

21st round (inc round) *Work 11 V sts, between next 2 V sts work a double V, rep from * to end. Join as before.

22nd round As 14th.

Work 2 rounds V st without shaping.

25th round (inc round) *Work 12 V sts, between next 2 V sts work a double V, rep from * to end. Join as before.

26th round As 14th. Fasten off.

Borders
Using No.1.50 (ISR) hook and No.10 cotton, rejoin yarn to join of 26th round.

1st round *2dc into 2ch sp of V st, 1dc into sp between V sts, rep from * to end. Join with a ss to first dc.

Work 3 more rounds dc.

5th round *1dc into each of next 6dc, 5ch, take hook out of working loop and insert it into the first of the 6dc, draw the working loop through and complete a dc, into the 5ch loop make 12dc, rep from * to end. Join with a ss to first dc. Fasten off.

Using No.1.50 (ISR) hook and No.10 cotton, rejoin yarn to join of 1st round at top edge.

1st round Work 2dc into each ch sp to end. Join with a ss to first dc.

2nd round As 5th round of border for lower edge.

Rose spray trimming
Using No.1.50 (ISR) hook and No.10 cotton make a length of ch 35.5cm (14in) long for stem. Work a row of dc into each side of ch. Fasten off.

Large rose
Using No.1.50 (ISR) hook and No.10 cotton, work 2 Irish rose motifs as given in Chapter 13, but starting with 24dc instead of 18 and making 8 petals.

Medium rose
Work 2 motifs as given for large rose, working first 5 rounds only.

Leaf
Using No.1.50 (ISR) hook and No.10 cotton make 22ch.

1st row Into 7ch from hook work 1tr, *2ch, miss 2ch, 1tr into next ch, rep from * 3 times more, 2ch, miss 2ch, 1dc into last ch. Turn.

Next row 2ch, 3dc into first ch sp, 1dc into next tr, *3tr into next ch sp, 1tr into next tr, rep from * twice more, 3dc into next ch sp, 1dc into next tr, 7dc into first 6ch, cont down 2nd side of leaf, 1dc into next tr, 3dc into next ch sp, **1tr into next tr, 3tr into next ch sp, rep from ** twice more, 1dc into next tr, 3dc into last ch sp. Join with a ss to 2nd of first 2ch.

Next round Work 1dc into each dc and tr, working 3dc into 4th dc at top of leaf. Join with a ss to first dc, make 8ch, turn and work 1dc into 3rd ch from hook, 1dc into each of next 4ch, to form stalk. Fasten off.
Make another leaf in same way.

To make up
Press each piece under a damp cloth with a warm

Top : Delicate Irish crochet lampshade cover
Above : Glittery evening belt for a touch of class

iron. Arrange rose spray on background and st in place. Mount cover on buckram or parchment, or st on to ready made lampshade.

Evening belt
Size
4cm (1½in) wide by 76cm (30in) long, adjustable

Tension
18 sts to 10cm (3.9in) over dc worked on No.4.00 (ISR) crochet hook using yarn double

Materials
1 x 100 metres (110yd) ball of Twilley's Gold-fingering in each of 3 colours, A, B and C
One No.4.00 (ISR) crochet hook
One 4cm (1½in) buckle

Using No.4.00 (ISR) hook and 2 strands of A, make a ch the required length, having multiples of 3 ch plus 1 extra turning ch, e.g. 136ch.

1st row (RS) Into 3rd ch from hook work 1dc, 1dc into each ch to end, joining in 2 strands of B on last dc. Break off A.

2nd row Using B, 4ch, *yrh, insert hook into next dc and draw a loop through, yrh and draw through 2 loops on hook, *, rep from * to * into same dc, miss 2dc, rep from * to * twice into next dc, yrh and draw through all 5 loops on hook — called 1Cl —, **2ch, rep from * to * twice into same dc as 2nd half of last 1Cl, miss 2dc, rep from * to * twice into next dc and complete 1Cl, rep from ** to last dc, 1ch, 1tr into last dc joining in 2 strands of A. Break off B.

3rd row Using A, 1ch, 2dc into first 1ch sp, *1dc into top of 1Cl, 2dc into 2ch sp, rep from * to end, working last 2dc into turning ch loop. Break off A.

4th row With RS of work facing join in 2 strands of C to beg of 3rd row, 1ch, 1dc into first st (edge st), 1dc into each dc to end, 2dc into turning ch, do not turn but cont across short end of belt, 1dc into end of 3rd row, 2dc into end of 2nd row, 1dc into end of 1st row, cont along starting ch, 1dc into first ch, 1dc into each ch to end, 2dc into last ch, work across other short end as before. Join with a ss to first ch. Do not turn.

5th row Using 1 strand of C only, work in crab st round all edges, as given in Chapter 7. Fasten off.
Sew buckle to one end of belt.